BRIGHT NOTES

IVANOV AND OTHER WORKS BY ANTON CHEKHOV

Intelligent Education

Nashville, Tennessee

BRIGHT NOTES: Ivanov and Other Works

www.BrightNotes.com

No part of this publication may be used or reproduced in any manner whatsoever without written permission, except in the case of brief quotations in critical articles and reviews. For permissions, contact Influence Publishers http://www.influencepublishers.com.

ISBN: 978-1-645424-22-2 (Paperback)
ISBN: 978-1-645424-23-9 (eBook)

Published in accordance with the U.S. Copyright Office Orphan Works and Mass Digitization report of the register of copyrights, June 2015.

Originally published by Monarch Press.
Jane Wexford, 1965
2020 Edition published by Influence Publishers.

Interior design by Lapiz Digital Services. Cover Design by Thinkpen Designs.

Printed in the United States of America.

Library of Congress Cataloging-in-Publication Data forthcoming.
Names: Intelligent Education
Title: BRIGHT NOTES: Ivanov and Other Works
Subject: STU004000 STUDY AIDS / Book Notes

CONTENTS

1)	Introduction To Anton Chekhov	1
2)	Ivanov	25
3)	The Seagull	37
4)	Uncle Vanya	64
5)	The Three Sisters	90
6)	The Cherry Orchard	115
7)	Critical Commentary	142
8)	Bibliography	146

INTRODUCTION TO ANTON CHEKHOV

FAMILY AND EARLY LIFE

Anton Chekhov had a curious life. Neither his inner existence (his philosophy, morality, and genius) nor his public biography followed a consistent, predictable pattern.

He was born in 1860, in Taganrog - a nasty little seaport town in the south of Russia. His grandfather was a serf who through great toil purchased the family's freedom. His father rose to the lower middle classes through the acquisition of a general store - his profits came mostly from short-changing and short-weighting.

Chekhov's early life was marked by despotism and hardship. His father was a brutal disciplinarian who fanatically believed in rigid religious instruction for his children. Chekhov once wrote to his brother: "It is sickening and dreadful to recall the extent to which despotism and lying mutilated our childhood."

YOUTH

Young Anton's schooling was a series of miserable experiences. At the age of eight, he was sent to a one-room parish school run by the Greek merchants of Taganrog for the children of the poor. The ignorant and brutal schoolmaster so oppressed the young boy that he could not or would not learn even the alphabet. The following year he was sent to the local gymnazia, a combined grammar and high school. Between chores at home and at the grocery store he had little time for studies, and his school record was abysmal. When Anton was sixteen, his father's store went bankrupt, and to escape debtor's prison the family fled to Moscow, leaving Anton behind. To sustain himself, the young Chekhov took on tutoring and managed to complete school with reasonable success.

STUDENT DAYS

In 1879, he joined the family in Moscow and enrolled in the University medical school. But family life in Moscow was no better than it had been in Taganrog, and to keep them all alive he began to write "trash" (as he later called it) for cheap local publications. Comic stories, recipes, legends, jokes, vaudevilles, and farces were all in his repertoire during his medical student years.

In 1884, Chekhov received his medical diploma and set up practice in Moscow. But his patients were poor and his practice provided little livelihood. He continued to write for his income. Said Chekhov later of this dual life: "Medicine is my lawful wife and literature is my mistress. When I get fed up with one, I spend the night with the other. Though it is irregular, it is less boring this way, and besides, neither of them loses anything through my infidelity."

AS YOUNG WRITER

The humor, brilliance and sheer volume of Chekhov's output (in all he wrote 600 to 800 tales, novellas and plays) eventually gained for him public recognition. By 1886, he had become a popular writer with two published books of collected stories and a regular feature in a prestigious newspaper. Despite a theatrical fiasco (the production of *Ivanov*) his reputation as a brilliant young writer grew and in 1888, at the age of 28, he was awarded the Pushkin Prize for distinguished literary achievement (although he himself felt he was "a lilliputian like everybody else" in his accomplishments.)

UNPREDICTABLE ADULT

In 1890, with no apparent motive, Chekhov took off for a 6,000 mile trip by train, boat, sledge, and coach to a penal colony on the island of Sakhalin, near Japan. He stayed three months, collecting statistics, history, geography, and anecdotes for a book, which he eventually published in Moscow - it was a majestic failure. All the while he was writing farces, mood pieces, and realistic short stories and gaining a large and faithful following.

But he was still a doctor. Throughout his life, Chekhov periodically embarked on public-spirited health projects (organizing famine relief, supervising cholera centers, educating peasants), all the while claiming his total indifference to the people he was helping. This detached sympathy (the mark of a good doctor) is reflected in his creative efforts in a tender, compassionate objectivity.

FAILING HEALTH

Chekhov had been in poor health ever since his student days, but by 1892 his condition became alarming. On the urging of his doctor, he took his parents and siblings to a country estate in Melikhovo, near Moscow, in the hopes of leading a quieter, cleaner, calmer life in the country, He resumed his medical practice, Again the peasants were too poor to pay and again he was forced to write at a feverish rate in order to support the family.

The consumption worsened, but Chekhov disregarded all advice. He continued to travel all over Europe and to work at a frantic pace. Finally, in 1898, he was forced to abandon his practice of medicine and with much reluctance settled in the warm climate of Yalta, on the Black Sea.

MARRIAGE

Exiled from Moscow and the hubbub of city life, Chekhov continued with difficulty to turn out stories and plays. Late in 1898, when the newly formed Moscow Art Theater revived *The Seagull* (which had failed dismally two years earlier), his life took a new turn. He met the young actress, Olga Knipper, and after a lengthy courtship, mostly by mail, he married her in 1901. They passed their honeymoon at a health spa. The Chekhovs' married life was a weird one. Olga spent her time performing in Moscow, Anton spent his staying alive in Yalta.

LAST YEARS

By 1900, Chekhov was, after Tolstoy, the foremost figure in Russian literature. But his frequent travels to Moscow and the excitement attached to each production of his plays were taking their final, fatal toll. On the night *The Cherry Orchard* opened (January 17, 1904) Chekhov scarcely had the strength to stand through the ovation given him. On July 2 of the year he died in a

German health resort and his body was shipped to Moscow in a refrigerated car used for transporting oysters (a touch he would have enjoyed).

Chekhov once bitterly summed up his own life in advice given to a young fellow author: "Write a story of how a young man, the son of a serf, a former grocery boy, chorister, high school lad and university student, who was brought up to respect rank, to kiss priests' hands, to revere other people's ideas, to give thanks for every morsel of bread, who was whipped many times, who without rubbers traipsed from pupil to pupil, who used his fists and tormented animals, who was fond of dining with rich relatives, who was hypocritical in his dealings with God and men gratuitously, out of the mere consciousness of his insignificance - write how this youth squeezed the slave out of himself drop by drop, and how, waking up one fine morning, he feels that in his veins flows no longer the blood of a slave but that of a real man."

AS DRAMATIST

It is a common error to think of Chekhov as a short-story writer who late in his career began experimenting with the drama. As a very young man Chekhov was fascinated by the dramatic form, but the conditions prevailing in the Russian theater were so discouraging (poor acting, uninspired direction, adherence to conventional melodrama and contrived **realism**) that an imaginative playwright would have little chance of staying alive, and no chance of supporting a family.

While still in high school, Chekhov wrote a full-length play (which has not survived). And during his second year in medical school he composed a very long, four-act play which was not published until 1923 and is known in English as

That Worthless Fellow Platonov. It is not a very good play, but it contains rudiments of some of his later themes, devices, and characterizations. During his early medical-school days, Chekhov wrote at least one more full-length and a one-act play, neither of which has ever turned up in his papers.

FIRST PRODUCTION

In 1887, when Chekhov, at twenty-seven already had some reputation for his short stories and vaudeville plays, the manager of a Moscow theater requested him to write a full-length play. The result of this request was *Ivanov*. Although it did not make much of a stir in Moscow, when it was performed later that year in St. Petersburg it met with great acclaim.

The success of *Ivanov* encouraged Chekhov to try his hand again at a full-length play. And in 1889, he submitted *The Wood Demon* to the Petersburg Dramatic and Literary Committee. It was rejected peremptorily. After much revision, Chekhov found a Moscow producer for the play and when it was performed in December, 1889, it was a total flop.

From then until 1895, Chekhov's disdain for the popular theater of his time triumphed over his urge to see his plays produced. Although he did churn out his delightful one-act farces (*The Bear, The Proposal, The Wedding, The Anniversary*) he publicly eschewed serious, full-length dramas.

THE SEAGULL

Then, in 1895, he suddenly wrote his friend, the publisher Suvorin: "Just imagine, I'm writing a play." This play was *The*

Seagull. Chekhov had been quietly taking it up and putting it aside for three years. As early as March, 1892, he wrote to Suvorin about a new play he envisioned, and in June of that year he wrote: "I have an interesting subject for a comedy, but I haven't thought of its ending so far. He who can invent new endings for a play, will start a new era. I can't get those endings right! The hero has either to get married or shoot himself."

The Seagull, too, when it was performed in 1896, was a major disaster. And this time Chekhov swore: "Never will I write these plays or try to produce them, not if I live to be 700 years old."

But fortunately, at that moment a new force entered the theatre scene - the Moscow Art Theatre. Formed for the very purpose of producing "misunderstood" plays like Chekhov's, the Art Theater provided the playwright a "home" for his dramatic talents.

FULL-FLEDGED DRAMATIST

From then on, starting with the brilliant revival of *The Seagull*, in 1898, Chekhov was a bonafide playwright. In October, 1899, the revised version of the miserably received *Wood Demon*, renamed *Uncle Vanya*, was produced with great success.

This was followed a year later (January, 1901) with a moving production of *The Three Sisters*. And finally, in 1904 (the hiatus was due to ill health and creative difficulties, not to abstinence from the theater), the masterpiece - *The Cherry Orchard*.

From his teens, Chekhov was alternately fascinated and repelled by the theater (he once called fiction his "legal wife" and the stage "a noisy, impudent and tiresome mistress"). And it was the conditions of the theater not Chekhov's unawakened interest which made him an "end-of-life" dramatist.

MOSCOW ART THEATER

John Gassner, the modern critic, writes that: "On June 21, 1897, there occurred a historic eighteen-hour conversation between two lovers of the theater who wanted to reform it. These were the critic and playwright Nemirovitch-Dantchenko and the amateur actor Constantin Stanislavsky." These two determined to form a theater group that rehearsed meticulously, that encouraged the actor to create his role as if it were at one with his personality, and that fostered an inner **realism** beyond the hackneyed, photographic, external attempts which were popular.

The Theater's first two productions, in 1898, almost ruined the enterprise. Then Dantchenko persuaded Chekhov to exhume *The Seagull*, and from near collapse a flourishing theater was born. For the rest of his life Chekhov worked closely with the Theater, and his plays have remained a stable part of its repertoire.

In deference to the wild success of *The Seagull* when it opened on October 17, 1898, and to the importance of Chekhov's plays for the continuation of the group, the Moscow Art Theater adopted the seagull as its permanent emblem.

THE NEW METHOD

Stanislavsky and Dantchenko rebelled successfully against the deathgrip of the stultified Russian theater. Under their new system, leading actors could no longer lay down the law and hog the entire limelight. Productions must be unified in respect to acting, dress, scenery, properties, music, and acting styles. And most of all, actors must not declaim but perform naturally and sincerely. These new rules were so perfectly suited to Chekhov's original dramatic style that, although the directors and playwright did not always agree on interpretation, the overall accord was so great as to foster at once a brilliant dramatist and a brilliant theater.

CHEKHOV'S RUSSIA

In 1861, the year after Chekhov was born, Tsar Alexander II bowed to the pressure of the liberals and authorized the emancipation of the serfs. In a decade of reform, the old autocratic system, with its police censorship, gave way to a reorganization of justice, a large measure of self-government, and the emancipation. But the new measures had not been prepared for - there was little accumulated capital, a tiny educated middle class, little experience in industry, commerce, and self-administration, and a lack of technical skills and resources.

With an attempt on the emperor's life in 1866, the government grew more and more reactionary and as a result the revolutionary movement spread wider and wider. By the late 1870s terrorist movements had sprung up everywhere. In 1881, when Chekhov was at medical school, Alexander II was finally assassinated.

Alexander III ruled in the 80s with extreme reaction and a vigorous police rule, and most of the concessions made during the age of reform were gradually revoked. Nationalism, Orthodoxy, and Autocracy were the bywords of the government. But Alexander's (and later Nicholas II's) autocracy could not stem the tide of onrushing Westernization, industrialization, and Marxism.

The men who were paralyzed by failure and hopelessness in the 80s began to gain new strength in the 90s, and by 1905, a year after Chekhov's death, they were optimistic and energetic enough to revolt.

CHEKHOV'S CHARACTERS

It is mostly the disappointed gentry of the 80s and 90s about whom Chekhov writes in his plays; the people who could not adjust to the new, repressive form of life, who were alienated from their old isolated grandeur, and were pessimistic about a changing future - a future perhaps dreamed about in the 60s and 70s, but now seemingly generations away.

PERSONAL PHILOSOPHY

Chekhov had no particular political or religious philosophy, and he himself said that he changed his outlook every month. At one period, for six or seven years, he was greatly touched by Tolstoy's philosophy of asceticism, but he soon rejected it, along with all other codified answers to life. In 1894, Chekhov wrote: "I am sick of theorizing of all sorts."

Chekhov has variously been accused of being anti-semitic (and yet he vigorously defended Zola in the Dreyfus case), of being unsympathetic to the lower classes (and yet in his plays he mercilessly satirizes the gentry), of forecasting the revolution (and yet at his death less than a year before it came he did not believe a revolution was in the making). Chekhov was an artist, not a philosopher or political scientist. He wrote about the world he observed around him and made no final judgments.

LITERARY INFLUENCES

When Chekhov first broke into print in a humor magazine (1880) the literary giants of the nineteenth century were still alive - Dostoyevsky, Turgenev, and Tolstoy. But the young medical student from serf backgrounds had little in common with these successful, cultured landed gentry. Chekhov found Dostoyevsky morbidly distasteful. Tolstoy's extremist theories fascinated him for awhile, but Tolstoy had already turned his back on art, and Chekhov, who was nothing if not an artist, had little to learn from the philosophical master. Gogol's humor and Turgenev's compactness surely served as accomplished examples for the young writer, but as Ernest Simmons the biographer notes: "Chekhov was much less of an imitator of anything that had gone before than a brilliant innovator, in form and content, initiating a new development in Russian literature."

THE NEW DEVELOPMENT

The conventional pre-Chekhov Russian play moved from one emotional crisis to the next while the audience was treated to a sensational succession of fights, quarrels, confessions, adulteries, suicides, murders, and the like. Chekhov adjured this superficial form of the drama. In one of his most famous letters (written as early as 1887) he formulated his revolutionary position:

"The demand is made that the hero and heroine should be dramatically effective. But after all, in real life people don't spend every minute shooting each other, hanging themselves and making confessions of love. They don't spend all their time saying clever things. They're more occupied with eating, drinking, flirting and talking stupidities - and these are the things which ought to be shown on the stage. A play should be written in which people arrive, go away, have dinner, talk about the weather and play cards. Life must be exactly as it is. And people as they are - not on stilts. . . . Let everything on the stage be just as complicated, and at the same time just as simple as it is in life. People eat their dinner, just eat their dinner, and all the time their happiness is being established or their lives are being broken up."

This credo is extremely exacting if a playwright it to sustain interest and present any kind of drama on the stage. It took Chekhov himself many years to perfect his "life as it is" technique, and in his earlier plays he was unable to purge his works completely of their outward melodrama.

OVERT MELODRAMA

In *Ivanov*, Chekhov's first produced play, we find the rudiments of his later perfected techniques, but we also find much of the old-fashioned melodrama. Acts II, III, and IV end respectively in a discovered illicit embrace, a cruel pronouncement of fatal disease, and a suicide. *The Seagull's* Act I, III, and IV curtains are no less sensational: a passionate confession of unrequited love, again an illicit embrace, and again a suicide. As he moves on to *Uncle Vanya* the overt melodrama begins to be submerged. There is a first-act confession of love, a third-act discovery of an illicit embrace and a climactic, but unsuccessful, shooting. But in *Vanya* the melodramatic stage business does not ultimately affect the action. Nothing changes as a result of the declaration, discovery, or shooting.

With *The Three Sisters* external melodrama nearly vanishes. The illicit-love declaration is reduced to a phrase of a song sung in public and the only shooting takes place way offstage, almost out of hearing.

Finally, in *The Cherry Orchard*, nothing remains of the old style of activity. No pistol shots (only the dull thud of the axes in the distance), no love complications, no deaths. Life in *The Cherry Orchard* is exactly as complicated and as simple as it is in real life.

HIDDEN MELODRAMA

However much he deplored the phony, contrived theatricality of his contemporaries, Chekhov was fully aware that a play without drama is no play at all. Ridiculous and paradoxical epithets of "undramatic" and "antitheatrical" have been hurled at Chekhov's plays. But they have been hurled by people unable to see the plot beneath the action, the tension beneath the card games, dinners, and idle chatter.

If we look at the stories (and despite the thoughtless accusations, there are stories) behind the action, we will find concealed not only strong drama, but indeed heavy melodrama. In *The Seagull* we have an aging actress losing her lover and selfishly destroying her son. We have an innocent young girl seduced, abandoned, and losing her child and then reduced to the sordid life of a provincial actress on tour. We have an aspiring young writer mutilated in spirit by his mother, deprived of his great love, unsuccessful in his work, and finally desperate enough to shoot himself. That none of this happens directly before our eyes is not to say it is not happening at all in the play.

In *Three Sisters* we have the great underlying melodrama of dispossession. The Prozoroffs are slowly dispossessed of their spirit and more concretely of their love. The moribund and sinister forces of the insensitive and uncultured provincials (embodied in the evil Natasha) eventually wear out and finally turn out the Prozoroffs. At first it is merely a matter of being forced out of their rooms and changing their habitual way of life. But by the end they are forced completely out of their house. Masha returns to Kulygin, Olga lives in town in a government apartment, Irina is going to live at the brickyard, and Andrei is kept busy out of the house pushing the baby carriage. In their places are the dispossessors - Natasha and her lover Protopopov. With the Prozoroffs evicted from their own home, Natasha will cut down some trees, change some furniture, and eradicate all traces of her antagonists. Once again, the essential drama is submerged. We do not see the dispossession taking place and yet what we do not see is the very center of the play - it is what the play is about.

Uncle Vanya is about an even more subtle dispossession - that of hopes and ideals. Through all the chatter and diversion we are seeing a family and their friends losing everything for which they lived and worked. And in *The Cherry Orchard*, the play in which the least action takes place onstage, we find the greatest melodrama of all - an entire generation and class turned out and homeless, alienated in a changing world, left without a familiar signpost or tradition.

HIDDEN TENSIONS

The tension and drama hidden away in Chekhov's plays is almost unbearable. It is the tension of people being dispossessed of home, ideal, spirit, love, meaning. But what we see on the stage is not the great undertheme (any more then we see it in real life as we move about our daily routine). What we see is unexceptional people leading mundane lives while beneath, beyond, behind them these dreadful things are happening.

CHEKHOV'S REALISM

It is this minute portrayal of life as it is which defines Chekhov's new approach to **realism**. One of the most famous (and apropos) examples of this **realism** comes in the fourth-act card game of *The Seagull*. While cards are being dealt, bids are being made, and the play is proceeding, it looks like an ordinary, friendly group of people passing the long autumn evening with a game of lotto. An essentially boring activity to watch on the stage, if that were all that were going on. But much, much more is happening. The underlying **themes** of the play are one by one being exposed between the bids and deals: Arkadina, who deludes herself with the thoughts that she is an important, triumphant actress, relives a recent trivial success before a bunch of students; Konstantine still has not met with literary success, and the others discuss his shortcomings: Arkadina has never yet found time to read her son's work (nor did she ever have time to do anything for him but drain his emotions); Shamreyeff mentions the stuffed seagull (the immolated Nina) which Trigorin has ironically forgotten (as he has forgotten Nina); Konstantine is uneasy and full of premonitions (lending a suspense which will resolve itself in his suicide that night).

It is nothing but an evening's card game on the surface. But the turmoil beneath builds a fierce drama and tension.

Another clear and painful example of the subsurface tension comes in the brief fourth-act exchange in *The Cherry Orchard* between Varya and Lopahin. Lopahin has just promised Mme. Ranevskaya that he will finally propose to her daughter Varya. Varya has been waiting for this proposal for two years. When the two are left alone they talk of the weather and of a broken thermometer and not one word is said about marriage. It is probably the most distressing conversation about the weather in drama.

COUNTERPOINT

One of the remarkable methods that Chekhov developed to maintain his lifelike surfaces with the seething understructures, was the use of the verbal counterpoint. Characters spin off into their own worlds of misery. They conduct intelligent conversations during which no one listens to anyone else. Individuals talk on about their own preoccupations as though each had been answered appropriately.

In the second act of *Three Sisters* there is a wonderful example of this counterpoint. People begin to arrive home from their day's activities and each one talks about the subject most on his mind, regardless of what he hears (or manages not to hear) the others saying. Vershinin is hungry, and when he doesn't get something to eat he complains about his wife and philosophizes about life - and no one is at all interested. Irina can talk only about her utter exhaustion. Tusenbach has resigned his commission but it is of moment only to himself. Masha is absorbed with the howling in the chimney and the melancholy it evokes in her.

They appear to be a group of people exchanging information about their day, but there is no practical exchange. They are talking at each other and over each over. The surface looks like a realistic bit of conversation. But the counterpoint is subtly evoking a mood of distraction and preoccupation.

MEANS OF CREATING MOOD

Chekhov uses many other means of creating mood - of putting the audience in the same frame of mind as the characters. One of his pet methods, frequently lost on modern readers of translations, is reference to other works and authors. It is as if in a contemporary play a character referred to Tennessee Williams. The theater audience would immediately, almost unconsciously, call up an image of a decaying and sordid south. And this image or frame of mind would be applied to the onstage atmosphere the playwright is attempting to create.

So Chekhov quotes liberally from folksongs and poems and from Shakespeare (in the first act of *The Seagull*, Konstantine and his mother trade lines from *Hamlet* - a way of defining their own relationship). He makes use, for his own atmosphere, of the images called up by Tolstoy, Gogol, Lermontov, Turgenev, etc. And the immediate responses these names (or specific works) call up are deftly applied to heighten tension, create suspense, or intensify a feeling.

STAGE SOUNDS

A more direct way of creating mood is Chekhov's liberal use of onstage and offstage sounds. He uses sound on two levels. One level is the obvious and conscious noise connected with the action. So we have the piercing, shattering fire alarm in Act III of *Three Sisters* (Chekhov worked for many hours to get just the right sound for that alarm). And at the end of the play there is the military music fading into the distance - one of the most nostalgic of public sounds.

In *The Cherry Orchard* we hear the famous distant and dull thud of the axes against trees. In *Uncle Vanya* we hear the sound of the carriage bells as everyone departs, leaving Sonia and Vanya once again in their desolate isolation. In *The Seagull* we hear Konstantine playing his melancholy waltzes from another room.

INCIDENTAL SOUNDS

As numerous as the action-connected noises are, there are a host of incidental sounds which less obviously create atmosphere. We frequently hear, for instance, the watchman tapping outside, closing the characters safely into their isolated worlds. Much use is made of music. Telegin plays his mournful guitar; the "Jewish orchestra," playing at the mock ball in *The Cherry Orchard*, plays numbers appropriate to the emotions revealing themselves in the next room; an officer strums his guitar at the three sisters' party.

Stanislavsky discusses how important sound is for a director of Chekhov's plays. "I invented all sort of mises en scene [staging] the singing of birds, the barking of dogs, [noises of] cuckoos, owls, clocks, sleigh bells, crickets."Chekhov himself liberally provided in the stage directions for noises of all sorts which contributed to his desired atmosphere.

USE OF NATURE

Chekhov used nature much in the way he used sounds - to further the mood he was creating. In *The Seagull*, for example, the first act is very much governed by the rising moon which is to provide the lighting for the disastrous theatrical. The last act of that play is dominated by a howling storm which causes the "bare and hideous" stage, used long ago at the theatrical, to shake and the curtains to flap. The wind howls in the chimney in *The Three Sisters*, evoking mournful memories. In *Uncle Vanya* the wind bangs the windows so violently that they have to be closed - shutting out all revivifying breaths of air.

Chekhov uses the local specifics of nature extensively. Think, for instance, how he uses trees. In Vanya the debased forests in the provinces are directly equated with the lives of the provincial inhabitants. In *The Three Sisters*, Natasha will chop down the old fir trees to complete her triumph of dispossession; in *The Cherry Orchard*, the blooming tress recall a flood of childhood memories condemned to the axe.

SEASONS

As much as he utilizes the specific, Chekhov also calls on the universal - the cyclical changes of the seasons. Through each play there is a progression of season corresponding to the action. Looking at *Three Sisters* for example, we find a perfect correspondence. The play opens with hope and some happiness - it is May 5. In the second act all is bleak and cold, the chill of their atrophied lives is enshrouding the characters - it is mid-January. And when the play ends, with the sisters turning their worn-out hope toward a cheerless winter of life, it is autumn and the birds of passage are already flying south.

The terminal note of all four major plays is similar. And Chekhov sounds each of these notes in the melancholy of autumn. Konstantine shoots himself on a night when they are playing cards to pass the long autumn evening. Astroff will not return to Vanya's house until the snow of the coming winter has gone; Lyuboff and her family finally leave their estate on an October afternoon.

TIME OF DAY

In much the same way Chekhov uses the hours of the day. Looking again at *The Three Sisters*, we go full cycle through the day. The first-act party takes place on a bright May day at noon. As darkness comes into their lives, in the second act, it is 8:00 P. M. of a winter's night. As their lives erupt during the fire, it is that dreadful hour, three in the morning. And at last, as the officers leave, it is again twelve noon - and how strongly we feel the difference between the opening and final noons.

The hour of the day is very much a part of the atmosphere of each act. Think, for instance, of the middle-of-the-night sleeplessness in Act II of *Vanya*. Everyone is edgy, tired, worn-out- how well the hour fits the action. Think of the blazing midday sun reflecting off the lake in *The Seagull's* second act. The noontime heat perfectly coincides with the boredom, lethargy, and idleness. Chekhov was very specific about the time of day, and he places constant reminders throughout the action of the hour and all the atmospheric implications of that hour. In the first act of *The Cherry Orchard* we hear countless times that the night is almost over. The opening two lines set the hour, and the exhausted family reminds each other endlessly how very late it is.

TIME PASSING

As precise as he is about the time of day, Chekhov is vague, almost obscure, about the amount of time between days, months, and years. We are given occasional signposts of the passage of time (the age and number of Natasha's children, the reference to seasons, mention of a trip just completed). But Chekhov's plays are, for the most part, suspended in time. These people, tucked away in the provinces, spend each day exactly like the one past and the one to come. This is the very horror of their lives. In *Uncle Vanya*, for instance, we are confused whether the second-act night time vigil occurs on the same day as the play opened or on a night a few weeks later. In the first act we hear Elena, Sonia, Serebriakoff, and Telegin chatting as they return from a walk (and a few moments later Elena and Sonia go into the house together). And yet, in the second act, Elena complains that Sonia is angry at her and "hasn't spoken to me for two weeks now." So, perhaps, at least two weeks have passed between the acts. In the first act Elena says she has not "really talked to" Astroff even once, and she has only seen him three times in her life. And yet, in the second act she knows all about his "bravery," his "genius," the details of his life, what he believes in. So perhaps she has had much more than two weeks to get to know the doctor. But to contradict this estimate of elapsed time is the continuity of the action itself. Astroff has come on the day the play opens to minister to Serebriakoff's ills. But now that Astroff has traveled all that distance, Serebriakoff seems quite well, he seems to be over his pains of the night before. He will not be examined. But Astroff announces his intention to spend the night anyway. The situation is exactly the same in the second act. Serebriakoff's night pains have returned and he is berated for turning away the doctor that day.

The problem is, then, is this the same attack of rheumatism, or has the doctor been summoned several times to tend to the hypochondriac who will not be treated? As long as we sense that these attacks and the conversations surrounding them have been going on interminably, it does not matter exactly which day it is. In fact, by obscuring the specifics, Chekhov contributes to the atmosphere of endless and utter tedium.

ARRIVALS AND DEPARTURES

In a world hemmed in by routine and boredom, arrivals and departures provide a great deal of excitement. In the four major plays the structure hangs on arrivals and departures. In *Three Sisters*, the arrival of Natasha starts the action, the departure of the regiment ends it. In *The Seagull*, the arrival of Arkadina and her lover starts the action, their departure temporarily ends it, their return renews it (as well as Nina's return). In *Vanya*, the arrival of the Serebriakoff's starts off Vanya's "discovery"; the departure of the Serebriakoff's restores the old order - with the poignancy of new, hopeless wisdom. *The Cherry Orchard* bustles at the outset with Ranevskaya's arrival and ends with a thud at her departure. Major comings and goings provide a perfect dramatic means for bringing all the characters together, for catching up with news (which provides the audience with **exposition**) and for revealing how various people feel about those coming and going. Chekhov was a master at exploiting every possibility of this dramatic device.

CHEKHOV'S MESSAGE

As a dramatist, and from all reports as a man, Chekhov had no final solution to the problems of life. Mistaken critics sometimes insist that his plays bear the message: "men must work to be happy." But look at the characters in his play who put forth that message: the drunken, boorish steward Borkin in *Ivanov*; the overworked, burnt-out Astroff and the contemptible professor in *Vanya*; the silly, ineffectual Baron in Three Sisters; and the fatuous perpetual student in *The Cherry Orchard*. This hardly sounds like a cast of characters a playwright would conceive to represent his own serious solutions.

Quite simply, Chekhov did not have a message. He was showing life as he saw it during the social and philosophical milieu of his day. His characters are carefully composed amalgams of the gentry and provincials of his time. Each one rings perfectly true as a character. Inherent in many of the ironic satiric characterizations is an implied criticism of certain human and class weaknesses. But it is not a specific human or a specific class. Chekhov's detached and observant eye looked with gentle amusement and genuine sympathy on the fault-riddled characters he created. He did not judge them. He did not offer suggestions on how to improve them. This is why Chekhov's major plays end neither happily nor wholly tragically. He did not presume to have the answers to the questions he posed.

RUSSIAN NAMES

Readers unfamiliar with the Russian system of nomenclature will find the multitude of names allotted to each character somewhat confusing. Generally a Russian male has three names: his first name, his patronymic (his father's name), and his last name. Thus we might have an imaginary character named Alexander Nikolaevich Chukovsky (Alexander, son of Nikolay Chukovsky). He might be referred to throughout a play in any one of the following ways:

Surname alone: Chukovsky

First name and surname: Alexander Chukovsky

First name and patronymic: Alexander Nikolaevich

First name and abbreviated patronymic: Alexander Nikolaevich

Abbreviated patronymic alone: Nikolaevich

First name alone: Alexander

French form of first name: Alexandre

Affectionate nicknames: Shura, Shurochka, Sashka, Sasha, Sashenka, etc.

The name problem is further complicated by disagreement among translators. Alexander may be transliterated as Aleksandr; Nikolay may appear as Nicholas, Nikolai, Nicholay; Chukovsky may look like Tchuhovsky, Chukoffsky, Tchukovsky, or Chuhoffsky.

To add to the confusion, women have their own, feminine endings. Thus Alexander's wife would be Sonia Andreevna Chukovskaya (Sonia, daughter of Andrey, wife of Chukovsky). Alexander's daughter would be Maria Alexandrovna Chukovskaya (Maria, daughter of Alexander Chukovsky).

It is worth a few moments before reading a Russian play to get each of the characters straight and to review mentally the names by which they might be designated.

IVANOV

INTRODUCTION

Except for a youthful, posthumously published attempt, *That Worthless Fellow Platonov*, Chekhov did not try his hand at serious full-length plays until 1887. With his keen sense of the dramatic and his infallible ear for dialogue, Chekhov's talents were ideally suited for the theater. But the mediocrity of the contemporary plays and performances had always inspired his contempt. As he wrote to a friend: "I don't want to have anything to do with the theaters nor with the public. To hell with them!" Nonetheless, when F. A. Korsh, manager of the Korsh Theater, requested Chekhov to write a full-length play, the temptation proved irresistible.

As Chekhov wrote to his brother Alex: "I wrote the play unexpectedly, after a certain conversation with Korsh. Went to bed, thought up a **theme**, and wrote it down. I spent less than two weeks on it."

On November 19, 1887, *Ivanov* had its premiere in Moscow. The prompter for the performance told Chekhov that in his thirty-two years of service he had never witnessed such excitement in the audience or behind the scenes. Loud hissing competed with foot stamping and applause. Blows were exchanged at the refreshment bar. And the police had to escort out of the theater two vociferous opponents of the play's merits. For all this, *Ivanov* did not create much of a stir with the Moscow public or reviewers. Audiences did not seem to grasp the character Chekhov was exposing in the exhausted *Ivanov*.

During the following year Chekhov substantially revised the play, saying to his friend, the publisher Suvorin: "If the audience leaves the theater with the conviction that Ivanovs are scoundrels and Doctor Lvovs are great men then I'll have to give up the theater and send my pen to hell."

Fortunately, Chekhov did not have to throw away his pen. When *Ivanov* opened again, this time in St. Petersburg, "its success was colossal, the kind of success which rarely happens on our stage," wrote the Petersburg Gazette.

Chekhov's later masterpieces have, for the most part, completely overshadowed this early, somewhat tendentious attempt to show "life as it is." His dream of "summing up all that has hitherto been written about whining, miserable people, and with my Ivanov saying the last word" was not fully realized in his first produced play. *Ivanov* is not, like his later plays, a brilliantly executed piece of drama. Its construction is somewhat flabby, its climaxes melodramatic and contrived, and in all the play is too talky. Nevertheless, we find in *Ivanov* an imaginative break with the traditional, action-packed, sermonizing pieces which plagued the Russian theater at the end of the nineteenth century.

The genius which was, within the decade, to make itself felt in *The Seagull* was already making audible attempts to be recognized.

CHARACTERS

Nikolai Ivanov

A thirty-five-year-old bankrupt landowner who is exhausted by the intellectual and reformist activities undertaken in his youth.

Anna Petrovna (Sarah)

Ivanov's wife. Daughter of a rich Jewish landowner who has disowned her.

Matvey Shabyelsky

Ivanov's uncle. A long-since bankrupt count in his sixties, who is supported by Ivanov on his estate.

Yevgeny Lvov

An earnest young doctor who will voice his righteous sentiments at any cost.

Pavel Lebedev

Chairman of the County Council. A sweet, ineffectual drunkard henpecked by a rich wife.

Zinaida Lebedev

A penny-pinching shrew who tyrannically rules her house and family.

Sasha Lebedev

The councilman's intelligent, emancipated young daughter who falls in love with Ivanov's helplessness.

Mihail Borkin

Ivanov's hard-drinking steward who spends his time devising dishonest plans for making money.

Marfa Babakina

A lonely and rich young widow.

Dimitri Kosich

A tax official in the neighborhood.

Avdotya Nazarovna

A neighboring old woman.

Yegors

A friend of the Lebedevs'.

Pyotr

Ivanov's servant.

Gavrila

Lebedev's servant.

Guests and visitors

ACT I

Nikolai Alexeyevich Ivanov is a thirty-five-year-old intellectual and liberal who has burnt himself out with all his causes and projects. Like so many intellectuals of his day he has lost heart with the scientific farming, new methods of education, and fervent speeches which fired his younger years.

He barely manages to support himself on his 1,000 acre estate and he hasn't a cent to his name. When he was thirty, Ivanov had fallen passionately in love with the daughter of a rich Jewish landowner. When they were married, his wife Sarah gave up her religion, her parents, and her money. After five years Sarah is still ready to sacrifice anything for Ivanov, but he no longer feels anything for her. On hearing from her doctor, Lvov, that Sarah is dying of tuberculosis, Ivanov mutters helplessly:

"And when you tell me she's going to die soon, I don't feel any love or even pity but a kind of emptiness, a king of fatigue."

Lvov, who is just out of medical school, is disgusted with the "heartless egoism and pitiless cruelty" he finds in Ivanov's neglect of his dying wife. The young doctor cannot understand the exhaustion and guilt which incapacitate Ivanov. Lvov prides himself on his outspoken frankness and honesty, but he is, in fact, boring and heartless in his narrow enthusiasms.

Ivanov is surrounded on his faltering estate by a drunken buffoon of a steward, Borkin, and his uncle Shabyelsky, a foolish parasite who has long since frittered away his fortune.

To escape the guilt and frustration of a decaying house, a dying wife and a life too soon broken by early causes, Ivanov frequently visits his neighbor Lebedev, to whom he is in debt for several thousand roubles.

ACT II

Lebedev himself is a drunken bumbler, thoroughly henpecked by his penny-pinching wife, Zinaida. Lebedev's daughter, Sasha, is an intelligent and emancipated young woman. One night, when Ivanov has come for another of the Lebedev's boring parties, Sasha flings herself at him: "I understand your problems. You're unhappy because you're lonely. You need someone to love, someone who understands you." Later that night, in wild abandon, Sasha confesses: "I'm madly in love with you.... You're my joy, my life, my happiness, the meaning to everything!" Ivanov is briefly stirred to his old passions: "Can it mean the beginning of a new life for me? Can it, Sasha? Oh, my happiness!" And just as he embraces her, Sarah appears in the doorway.

ACT III

Ivanov's state of self-contempt and despair is too deep to be altered by Sasha. The day after the kiss he has already given up all hope for a new life or new happiness. Lvov, in his blind "honesty," tries to shame Ivanov out of his melancholy and indifference: "You want [Sarah] to die, so you can be free. . . . Do you think you'd lose that girl and her money if you'd let your wife die naturally instead of bringing it on faster with your heartless cruelty? . . . You're such an impostor."

Ivanov, realizing what a mistake he made in encouraging Sasha, avoids her. Finally she indiscreetly comes to see him, begging for his affection: "Any girl would rather love a failure than a success, because she wants her love to accomplish something." Once again Sasha stirs Ivanov with her ardent devotion and admiration. In the meantime, Lvov the forthright tells Sarah of Sasha's visit and for the first time Sarah confronts Ivanov with his deceptive behavior. In a bitter quarrel Sarah accuses Ivanov of marrying her for her money and now, finding that her parents won't give them a cent, he has turned to another rich young girl to practice his deception. Ivanov responds to this fury with fury of his own: "Shut up, you Jew!" he screams. And later: "All right, you may just as well know the truth . . . you're going to die soon. The doctor told me that you're dying."

ACT IV

Within the year Sarah dies and Ivanov prepares to marry Sasha. Just before the ceremony Sasha confesses to her father that she has grown weary of Ivanov's complaining, guilt, and brooding. She is not sure she still loves him. Ivanov suddenly appears at the bride's house and tells Sasha: "I've been playing Hamlet and you've been playing a noble-minded young girl - but we couldn't keep this little charade up for very long." Ivanov feels that all his strength and energy are used up and even with Sasha's devotion they will never be renewed. As Sasha attempts to convince Ivanov that he will "live" again, Lvov rushes in and to all the assembled guests denounces Ivanov as a "worthless scoundrel."

Suddenly Ivanov takes out his revolver and cries: "I feel that my youth has been reawakened - the old Ivanov has spoken!" Before the startled guests can move he rushes out of the room and shoots himself.

Comment:

The **theme** of *Ivanov* was new to the Russian theater. The plays of the day were filled with pompous moralizing about the great social issues, but no one had ever written a drama, without sermonizing, about the demoralized men involved in these issues.

Ivanov is typical of the liberal intellectuals who feverishly threw themselves into the reform activities of the 1860s. Suddenly these men, at an early age, found as Ivanov did: "Without knowing my strength or any weakness, without even thinking, without knowing anything about life, I carried a load that was too much for me, and I broke under the strain."

But Ivanov cannot live with his broken self. He is plagued by unappeasable guilt, self-contempt, inertia, and boredom. He can find no joy or pleasure in the people around him. And everywhere he goes he brings a sense of gloom, despondency, defeat, and confusion.

To the self-righteous young Lvov, Ivanov gives advice that sounds like the sermonizing of an old man: "You're young and full of energy, while I'm thirty-five I have a right to give you advice. Don't marry Jewesses, or neurotics, or blue stockings, but choose a nice ordinary girl. . . . Just try to make your life as quiet as possible. . . . Don't try to fight the masses singlehanded, don't tilt with windmills, don't knock your head against brick walls."

When *Ivanov* was first produced in Moscow, the play was misunderstood. Actresses wanted to know why Ivanov should be such a scoundrel (which, of course, he is not); friends thought Lvov was a 'great man" (yet Chekhov derides his fatuous "integrity"). To explain himself, Chekhov wrote a long letter to his friend Suvorin defining exactly what he meant by the play.

"Ivanov," he wrote, "is a gentleman, a University man, and not remarkable in any way. He is excitable, hot-headed, easily carried away, honest and straightforward like most people of his class. . . . His past is beautiful, as is generally the case with educated Russians." But the burden such Russians undertake with excitement and fervor when they are young leaves them exhausted at thirty. "Conscious of physical exhaustion and boredom [Ivanov] does not understand what is the matter with him, and what has happened. . . . The change that has taken place in him offends his sense of what is fitting. He looks for the causes outside himself and fails to find them: he begins to look for them inside and finds only an indefinite feeling of guilt. It is a Russian feeling."

Added to this exhaustion, boredom, and guilt is loneliness. Ivanov's neighbors are drunkards, card players, and eager-beaver fools. None understands his great emptiness.

Piled on top of Ivanov's inner conflicts are the external demands of life. His wife is dying, his debts are enormous, and an emancipated young woman is flinging herself about his neck. Under pressures from within and demands from without Ivanov finally collapses from a self-pronounced sentence.

As for Lvov, Chekhov held him in the greatest contempt: "Anything like breadth of outlook or unreflecting feeling is foreign to Lvov. He is the embodiment of a program, a walking tendency. He looks through a narrow frame at every person and event, he judges everything according to preconceived notions."

Chekhov wrote the play not as an intellectual thesis or polemic but as the result of "observing and studying life." Later plays are to show the brilliant fruits of this recording and observing. As for *Ivanov*, it approaches but does not reach the pinnacle of psychological naturalism Chekhov was later to perfect. The young playwright, in 1887, was still partially bound by the theatrical **conventions** he was later to abjure.

For instance, each act has a "smash" curtain. Act I ends with Ivanov leaving Sarah to go to the Lebedev's and Lvov declaring excitedly: "No, I'm finished. I've had enough." The second-act curtain rings down on Sarah discovering Ivanov and Sasha in an embrace. Act III concludes with Ivanov's declaration to Sarah that she will soon die. And Act IV ends as Ivanov dashes off stage to shoot himself.

Chekhov never quite gave up the dramatic finale (*The Seagull* ends with Konstantine's suicide; *Three Sisters* ends with Tusenbach's death in a duel: *The Cherry Orchard* finishes with the sound of the axes chopping down the trees). But in later plays he was to develop a subtlety of characterization without resorting to public self-analysis and hackneyed melodrama. When Ivanov stands alone in Act III and declaims: "I'm a worthless, pitiful, contemptible man.... Oh, God, how I hate myself" and then goes on to tell the audience what is the matter, we see too clearly the hand of an inexperienced playwright. In the later plays, Chekhov will manage these insights through much more subtle and dramatic means.

Although Chekhov felt that he was depicting in *Ivanov* a peculiarly Russian sense of excitability, exhaustion, and guilt as embodied in the intellectuals of the 1860s, the brilliance of the play rests in its viability and applicability to zealous reformers as they burn themselves out eighty years after *Ivanov* was written.

ESSAY QUESTION AND ANSWER

Question: How does Chekhov's great sympathy for his characters display itself in *Ivanov*?

Answer: Although he is portraying a group of generally unsavory characters, Chekhov's prime concern lies not in exposing the individuals, but rather in relating the futile condition of their lives. Chekhov is extremely gentle and empathetic with the trapped Ivanov. He is at pains to show that far from being a scoundrel, Ivanov attempts to be extremely honest with himself and those around him. Two estimable women love Ivanov.

Sarah's descriptions of him when he was an ardent young reformer make him sound thoroughly attractive, and Sarah is the one wholly good character in the play. Sasha loves him for the wrong reasons, but she nonetheless sees in him a gentleness and manliness worth saving.

At no point do we receive the impression that Chekhov is criticizing *Ivanov*. His one great antagonist, Lvov, who publicly denounces him, is himself a less than admirable fellow and his denunciations are highly suspect.

Chekhov is saying of *Ivanov*: this is his condition, this is what life has made of him. But what can he do, poor fellow? Chekhov provides no answers, only the greatest tenderness and fairness in describing Ivanov's malaise.

THE SEAGULL

Seven years passed between the time Chekhov failed miserably with *The Wood Demon* (which was later transformed into *Uncle Vanya*) and before he produced a new drama, *The Seagull*. In the intervening years he wrestled with many ideas and put aside many false starts.

The inspiration for *The Seagull* came in an insignificant shooting expedition with Isaac Levitan, a well-known painter. Levitan winged a woodcock, which fell into a puddle. The sight of the surprised bird so distressed the two men that they finally killed it. "There was one beautiful creature less in the world," writes Chekhov, "and two fools went back home and sat down to supper." Chekhov's horror at this senseless destruction was later turned into one of the most moving scenes in *The Seagull*.

The Nina-Trigorin romance was lifted almost bodily from an earlier short story, *A Boring Story*. But the matter of plot was Chekhov's least concern. He was searching for a new way to present material on the stage and he was having difficulty putting his drama together. Then, in the summer of 1895, Levitan, who suffered from fits of depression and had several times attempted suicide, again tried to kill himself. Chekhov went to visit him at a large estate near the banks of a lake. The incident was apparently the missing piece for the drama which was so deeply puzzling Chekhov.

For in October, 1895, Chekhov wrote his friend, the publisher Suvorin: "Just imagine, I'm writing a play. . . . I'm writing it with pleasure though I sin terribly against the **conventions** of the stage. It is a comedy with three female parts, six male, a landscape (view of a lake), much talk about literature, little action, and tons of love."

Chekhov revised the play many times during the year, and then the Alexandrinsky Theater in Petersburg invited him to stage *The Seagull* as a benefit performance for a comic actress celebrating her twenty-fifth year on the stage. On October 17, 1896, *The Seagull* opened and it was an utter disaster. The first act was booed and hooted, and for the remainder of the play the audience laughed aloud at solemn moments and talked among themselves. Chekhov's biographer, Ernest Simmons, notes: "All agreed that nothing quite like this failure had ever happened before in the Russian theater." And Chekhov sneaked out of the theater with his coat collar up around his ears.

The play was left to its early grave for two years. Then the newly formed Moscow Art Theater bravely undertook to stage it. On December 17, 1898, pandemonium broke loose at the Art Theater. The first-night audience roared its approval, and overnight Chekhov the dramatist was launched.

The Seagull, in a very real sense, "made" the Moscow Art Theater. Under its famous director, Stanislavsky, the Theater went on to stage all of Chekhov's plays and, in gratitude, adopted the Gull as its emblem.

CHARACTERS

Irina Arkadina, Madame Trepleff

A well-known provincial actress in popular plays. She lives openly with her lover, Trigorin. At forty-three she retains her looks and vanity and thrives on her theatrical successes.

Konstantine Trepleff

Mme. Arkadina's son. A twenty-five-year-old aspiring and sensitive playwright supported by his uncle on an estate in the country.

Peter Sorin

Brother to Arkadina, uncle to Konstantine. A sixty-year-old retired civil servant, discontent with his dull life in the country.

Nina Zaryechny

Daughter of one of Sorin's wealthy neighbors. Young (eighteen or nineteen) and ambitious for a stage career. Loved by Konstantine and later Trigorin.

Boris Trigorin

An extremely famous, popular novelist in his late thirties. Lover of Mme. Arkadina and later Nina.

Ilya Shamreyeff

A retired lieutenant, now the close-fisted, tyrannical steward of Sorin's estate.

Pauline Shamreyeff

The steward's wife and mistress of Dr. Dorn.

Masha Shamreyeff

The steward's melancholy daughter, hopelessly in love with Konstantine, later wife of Medvedenko.

Eugene Dorn

A local doctor once the ladies' man of the neighborhood, now Pauline Shamreyeff's lover.

Semyon Medvedenko

A provincial schoolmaster supporting his family on a meager pension. Later Masha's husband.

Yakov

A laborer on Sorin's estate.

ACT I

Setting: A section of the park on Sorin's estate. An avenue leading to the lake is closed by a makeshift platform.

Konstantine Trepleff, a sensitive and emotional young man of twenty-five, is planning a theatrical for his friends and relatives on his uncle Sorin's estate. He has written the play, his first attempt to be presented publicly, to demonstrate his theories of what serious art should be. Nina, a lovely young neighbor with whom Konstantine is wildly in love, is to star in the play. It is her first appearance on the stage and she is highly nervous and anxious.

Konstantine's play is a natural and dramatic means for bringing all the characters together. And in bringing them together Chekhov introduces the complexities of their relationships.

The act opens with one of the most famous exchanges in modern drama:

Medvedenko: "Why do you always wear black?"

Masha: "I am in mourning for my life. I'm unhappy."

Medvedenko, a neighboring schoolmaster on a meager pension (of which he never tires complaining), lives with his mother, two sisters, and a younger brother. He supports them all but escapes for his pleasure to Sorin's estate where he courts (without success) the caretaker's young daughter Masha, Masha, for her part, torturously loves the uncaring Konstantine.

But Konstantine adores Nina, who lives nearby with a "beast" of a father and a selfish stepmother. Her parents have forbidden her to go to Sorin's, where she is drawn to the lake "like a seagull." She is greatly attracted by the glitter and intellectuality, and she must sneak out to perform in Konstantine's play. Nina does not return Konstantine's ardor. She dreams of a stage career, and at Sorin's she can meet a famous actress, a famous novelist, intellectuals, and landowners who stimulate her, frighten her, and might be of use to her in a stage career.

Sorin himself is one of those Chekhovian standbys who live on the "what might have beens." He might have married many times, but didn't. He might have written novels, but didn't. He might leave his hated country life, but doesn't.

Sorin's sister, Mme. Arkadina, is a well-known stage actress, visiting on her brother's estate. She and her son Konstantine are involved in an emotional and artistic conflict of Hamletean proportions. Arkadina jealously guards her reputation as a fine actress. She mocks her son's efforts to write a play and is hurt by his implied criticism of her superficial work. Konstantine has great contempt for his mother's popularized "art." As for her lover, Trigorin, a successful novelist in his thirties, Konstantine finds that "a little of Trigorin goes a long way."

As the moon rises over the lake, Konstantine calls everyone to sit down for the performance. The play is about life as it will be in 200,000 years. Nina, acting the "one living soul in the world," tells of the separation of spirit and matter through the centuries. After her long recitation, Arkadina begins to mock the play aloud. The others also begin to talk aloud among themselves. Konstantine, in a fury of disappointment, rings down the curtain and storms away. Arkadina acts surprised that her son has taken offense at her ridicule - after all he said it was all to be in fun and she hadn't expected to have to listen to metaphysics.

The other members of the audience are bored and uninterested except for Dr. Dorn. Dorn is a neighboring practitioner, witty and sympathetic. He had been moved by the intensity, freshness, and naivete of Konstantine's play, and he offers the distraught young man support and encouragement. As everyone disperses from the theater, Masha finds the sympathetic Dorn and anguishedly confesses her burning love for Konstantine. Dorn, overwhelmed by all the emotion he has witnessed, exclaims: "How nervous they all are! How nervous they all are! And so much love! O magic lake!"

Comment:

The act turns on the preparation, performance, and failure of Konstantine's play. Although the performance itself lasts only a few moments, the anxiety leading up to it and Konstantine's great despair afterward provide the tension of the act's movement.

There is a great sadness and tedium in the setting, in the atmosphere, in the people. And underneath the boredom is boiling frustration - frustration in love and in life. Medvedenko the schoolmaster is bound by poverty and family responsibility. He can think of little else but his need for money. After the play, which he has not understood at all, Medvedenko turns excitedly to Trigorin saying: "You know, somebody ought to put in a play, and then act on the stage, how we poor schoolmasters live. It's a hard, hard life." Medvedenko loves Masha in a plodding way. He realizes that "my soul and your soul can't find any ground to meet on"; but nonetheless he comes every day to offer his affection.

Masha, in black and in mourning for her life, is the rebel in a small town. She takes snuff and liquor with impunity, believes that "even a beggar can be happy," and revels in her tortured soul. Her love for Konstantine is passionate, futile, and shameless. She can find no kindred soul or mind among her provincial neighbors.

Sorin is frustrated to the point of inertia. Neither his life nor his locale suits him, and somehow he has let the years slide by in meaninglessness.

The pyramid of frustration, which climaxes in the artistic and emotional conflicts of Konstantine and his mother, has a broad base in the ennui of the other characters. Masha's mother, Pauline, in love with Dr. Dorn, is frantically jealous of Mme. Arkadina and the glamor surrounding her. Dorn, who was once the most sought - after gallant in the neighborhood, has become cynical and objective about his own and others' involvements.

But most of all, there is the great struggle between Arkadina and Konstantine. The mother, a popular, commercial performer, selfishly wants from her son the same love and approval she requires from her public and her admirers. The son, scornful of his mother's talents, has turned away from her and towards one who will replace her, young Nina. The mother is jealous. The son seeks, but cannot receive, approval from his mother. The mother seeks, but cannot find, admiration from her son. The tension, both covert and surface, is unbearable.

Chekhov also has used the play within the play as a means of expressing his own views about the theater. When *The Seagull* was written, the stage fare was a steady diet of conventional attempts at **realism**, action-packed melodramas, and psychologically false characterization throughout. Konstantine says of his mother's "holy art": "Her theater today is nothing but routine, **convention**. . . . When in a thousand different dishes they serve me the same thing over and over, over and over, over and over-will, it's then I run. . . . We must have new forms."

And yet, clearly, Chekhov does not approve of the "new forms" Konstantine has invented. His play has no "living characters in it" and his defense of this dearth is that "I must represent life not as it is and not as it should be, but as it appears in my dreams." Although Chekhov, too, is seeking new forms, what he seeks is to make characters ever the more real and true. He is not interested in presenting "some sweet little bit anybody can understand and any fool take home." But unlike Konstantine, he is concerned with the inner truths, the stratum beneath the protective covering of daily routine. Presentation of a playwright's dreams does not make good theater. Chekhov knew this, Konstantine did not. And through Konstantine's errors, Chekhov makes a strong complaint against the untruthful approach to drama.

ACT II

Setting: A croquet lawn. It is noon of a hot and still day. The lake is off to one side in the distance.

Much anger and anguish comes to the surface in this act. Masha, in a pathetic exchange with Arkadina, complains that she feels a thousand years old. "I trail my life along after me like an endless train . . . often I have no wish to be living at all."

Arkadina, for her part, feels "light as a bird" at forty-three. Even in the country her concerns are with her appearance and her domination of the scene. But she is bored and stifled with the "country dullness." Out of her boredom and the insufficient attention she is receiving, she has a bitter quarrel with Shamreyeff, steward of Sorin's estate. Arkadina had planned to drive into the city that day, but Shamreyeff has used all the horses, even the carriage horses, for hauling in the rye. Arkadina, furious at being crossed, screams: "What horses? How should I know . . . what horses!" And Shamreyeff retorts: "I am on my knees before your talent, I'd gladly give ten years of my life for you, but I cannot let you have the horses!" As the argument continues, Arkadina huffs that she will leave that day - if she has to walk to the station.

The explosion of anger brings everyone's tension to the surface. Sorin, whose inertia has left the sole management of the estate in Shamreyeff's hands, yells after the steward: "You insufferable man! Tyrant!" And then he retires to the house for an asthma attack.

Pauline, Shamreyeff's wife and Dorn's long-time mistress, complains to Dorn: "I can't bear his coarseness," and then she begs the doctor to "take me with you." At Dorn's gentle refusal, Pauline falls into a jealous rage and rips to shreds a bunch of flowers Nina had innocently given him.'

Nina, who has three days of "freedom" while her parents are off on a trip, is bewildered by the ordinariness of these illustrious people. Arkadina, a famous actress, is off weeping in the house over a pair of carriage horses. Trigorin, the darling of the public, takes his greatest pleasure in catching two chub. "I imagined famous people were proud and distant . . . but here I see them like everybody else."

Konstantine, who has been spending his days brooding on the lake, suddenly appears before Nina, and lays a dead seagull at her feet. Nina is repelled by Konstantine's strangeness and intensity. "And this seagull, I suppose that's a symbol, too. Forgive me, but I don't understand it."

Konstantine gives vent, in a rush, to all his bitterness. "This began that evening when my play failed so stupidly. Women will never forgive failure.... Your growing cold to me is terrible, unbelievable ... you despise my kind of imagination. You already consider me commonplace, insignificant." And as Trigorin approaches: "Here comes the real genius.... I won't stand in your way."

Trigorin, too, tells Nina of his dissatisfactions. "Day and night one thought obsesses me: I must be writing, I must be writing. ... I write incessantly and always at breakneck speed." Trigorin lives life only in terms of what it will provide for his novels and never in terms of his own pleasure. And yet his writing never pleases him: "To my dying day that's what it will be, clever and charming, charming and clever ... nothing more."

When Nina shows Trigorin Konstantine's dead seagull, the writer immediately and ominously jots in his notebook an idea for a short story: "A young girl, one like you, has lived all her life beside a lake; she loves the lake like a seagull and is happy and free like a seagull. But by chance a man comes, sees her, and out of nothing better to do, destroys her, like this seagull here."

As Trigorin hears from Arkadina that after all they are not to leave for the city that day, Nina steps forward and whispers: "It's a dream."

Comment:

Our insights into Mme. Arkadina during this act are not pleasant ones. She is a self-centered, false, and dangerous woman. She gloats to the miserable Masha: "The reason I have kept my looks is because I've never been a frump, never let myself go, as some do." And her fury at Shamreyeff for not providing her with horses for her pleasure is unreasonable and uncontrolled. She has neither sympathy nor concern for the labor which goes on at the farm - she is, after all, an artists, and these matters of toil and sweat are no concern of hers. Arkadina's satellites - Nina, Sorin, Pauline - sympathize with her wounded sensibility over the horses. A famous actress needs to be catered to.

Only Konstantine has avoided the magnetic field of the famous actress and her more famous lover - he has been brooding and melancholy, spending his time at the lake and not in the sparkling company. His mood is so low that from sheer wantonness he shoots a beautiful seagull. He is guilty about his senseless destruction, but he uses the dead bird as a means of threatening Nina: "It's the way I'll end my own life." The implication being, if you don't return my love I'll kill myself. Nina no longer has time for Konstantine. At best she never returned his ardor but now her relationship with the famous Trigorin is getting warmer and the insignificant Konstantine is nothing but a nuisance.

Nina is totally infatuated with the glamor surrounding Trigorin (how does it feel "being a famous genius?" she asks disarmingly). To her young eyes Trigorin has "a bright, interesting life that means something. You are happy." But Trigorin disabuses her of this notion. In a long speech, the writer confesses what his life is really like - and in this confession we hear much from another writer, Anton Chekhov. The obsessive, breakneck speed with which Trigorin turns out his charming but insignificant works is highly reminiscent of Chekhov's early days, when he churned out hundreds of pieces to support his family. Tolstoy said of Trigorin that he should never have been included in the play. "There aren't many of us [writers] and no one is really interested in us." Tolstoy considered Trigorin's long monologue about his art the best thing in *The Seagull* - and he was convinced it was autobiographical. But the monologue belonged in a letter or as a separate piece: "In a play it is out of place."

This speech and Trigorin's Act III exchange with Arkadina frequently lead to the misrepresentation of Trigorin. He is not a trivial, ineffectual dandy: he is first of all a writer of eminence. He is the current toast of the literary world, with a large and admiring following - to which both Arkadina and Nina belong. Chekhov's implied criticism of Trigorin comes in the lack of "iron in his blood" - a lack that Chekhov frequently condemned in the writers of his day. Trigorin may catch "with one stroke of [his] pen . . . what is typical of any person or landscape," but his stories lack a consciousness of aim. Trigorin is the first to admit this absence of purpose. Chekhov does not intend to write Trigorin off as a posing dandy - there is too much of Chekhov himself in the characterization. Trigorin, for instance, does not dress, as directors often make him, like a stuffy gentleman. Chekhov went to the trouble to explain: "He wore check trousers and his shoes were in holes." And he didn't even know how to smoke a cigar properly! Trigorin is wholly unselfconscious; he simply lacks genius.

At the end of the act, Chekhov gives us a signal that this "darling country dullness" is soon to be disastrously interrupted. As in his other major plays, Chekhov introduces a foreign element, in this case Arkadina and her lover, into a superficially tranquil environment, and the invasion causes great destruction. When Trigorin tells the rapt and infatuated Nina of his idea for a short story - the wanton destruction of a young girl - a sudden premonition comes over Nina and the audience. (In earlier versions of the play Chekhov filled the pause after Trigorin's ominous musings with: Nina (shudders): Please don't.") The man who comes "by chance" and wreaks destruction is the same invading element embodied in Trigorin and Arkadina. Only the latter invasion does not culminate, as we shall see, in utter destruction.

ACT III

Setting: A dining room in Sorin's house. In the middle of the room a table. A small trunk and hatboxes, signs of preparations for leaving.

A week has passed since Konstantine shot the seagull, and Arkadina is preparing to take Trigorin back to the city with her. Much has happened in that week. Masha has decided "to tear this love out of my heart by the roots" and is going to marry Medvedenko. She hopes when she's married that she "won't have any time for love." Konstantine has tried to shoot himself, and now he has challenged Trigorin to a duel. Nina is openly in love with Trigorin, and he now returns the infatuation.

The act is built around a series of "interviews" in Sorin's dining room. First Masha and Trigorin, who enjoy each other as drinking companions, bid farewell. Masha tells of her plans for marriage and asks him to autograph his books for her: "To Maria, who not remembering her origin, does not know why she is living in this world." When Masha leaves, Nina comes with a farewell present: a medallion inscribed with a page reference to one of Trigorin's books. Trigorin later looks up the reference. It reads: "If you ever, ever need my life, come and take it."

Arkadina and Sorin, left alone in the dining room, discuss Konstantine's attempt at suicide. Arkadina has "a notion the main reason was jealousy, and the sooner I take Trigorin away from here the better." Sorin knows of other reasons. Konstantine is lonely and bored in the country. He has no position, no money, no future, and no purpose. Sorin pleads with Arkadina to give her son some money so that he may be more than a useless dependent. But she replies: "Perhaps I could manage a suit, but as for going abroad . . . no. Just at this moment I can't even manage the suit. I haven't any money!" Later she admits: "Yes, I have some money, but I'm an actress, my costumes alone are enough to ruin me." Sorin and Arkadina's discussion is ended by one of his periodic fits of faintness, and then Konstantine enters with a bandage wrapped about his head.

At first, Konstantine and his mother are as tender as lovers with each other: "Mother, change my bandage. You do it so well." "Lately, these last days, I have loved you as tenderly and fully as when I was a child. Except for you, there's nobody left me now."

But the tenderness vanishes when Konstantine voices his fury at Trigorin. The writer had come between him and his mother and now between him and Nina. Mother and son argue from the depths of their confusion and pain. Arkadina accuses her son of envy: "People who are not talented but pretend to be have nothing better to do than to disparage real talents." Konstantine goads his mother with her lover's attraction for the adoring Nina. "You two with your stale routine . . . think that only what you do is real or legitimate. . . . I don't believe in you two," Konstantine bellows deprecatingly. "Decadent," screams Arkadina. "Kiev burgher! Sponge! . . . Beggar! Non-entity!" "Go back to your darling theater and act there in trashy stupid plays!" yells Konstantine. "Miser!" As they have always done, the two make peace and Konstantine agrees to drop his challenge of a duel. When Trigorin returns from looking up Nina's page reference, Konstantine leaves quickly to avoid him.

Between Arkadina and Trigorin the scene is explosive and somewhat comic. Trigorin asks to be freed so he can stay with Nina. Arkadina throws herself at his feet - "you are the last chapter of my life" -and claims him wholly for herself. "You are mine . . . you are mine." Muttering to himself, Trigorin consents to be carried away. "I have no will of my own . . . I've never had a will of my own."

With Trigorin in tow, Arkadina departs (giving as tip one rouble to be shared among the cook, the maid, and the workman). As Trigorin returns momentarily for his walking stick, he meets Nina alone. She says she will follow him to the city and take up an acting career. "I'm off like you . . . for Moscow . . . we shall meet there." He confesses his love for her and they kiss passionately.

Comment:

Since Chekhov's great plays are not dramas of action, but rather studies of "life as it is" -investigations of emotional states at a given point - the traditional third-act climaxes of action are nowhere in evidence in *The Seagull's* third act. What action there has been - Konstantine's attempted suicide, Masha's acceptance of Medvedenko's proposal, Nina and Trigorin's romance - has all happened offstage at another time. What we do find in the act are psychological climaxes in relationships. The title world into which each of the characters retreats has somehow been shaken and bruised by a colliding world and the result of each collision is shown in a two-by-two confrontation.

Trigorin and Masha's interview serves the dramatic function of **exposition**; it is not a psychological unveiling like the ones which follow it. Through their discussion we learn of Masha's decision to marry, of Trigorin's reluctant impending departure, of Konstantine's suicide attempt, and of his challenge to Trigorin.

Between Nina and Trigorin we are given a brief and graceful love scene with a heavy reminder of the dead seagull.

Sorin and Arkadina take up a discussion we are sure they have had many times before. Arkadina prefers not to hear Sorin's plea on behalf of Konstantine's pride and pocketbook. She has spent half her life depriving him both. Arkadina reveals her great selfishness and miserliness in her protestations of poverty -and she shortly follows this up with that wonderful one-rouble tip to be split three ways. Like all the men in her charmed circle, Arkadina's hypochondriacal brother is well in her power. He ultimately concedes: "You are very good, my dear. I respect you," although through mismanagement of his estate, he is also desperate for some of her hoarded cash.

The strength in the sister-brother exchange comes, as so often in Chekhov, in the unspoken. Sorin loves his nephew and would like to fight on his behalf against the destructive powers working against him. But Sorin is spineless, will-less, and juiceless. He can only complain to his manipulating sister, never make demands of her. Arkadina is perhaps a little ashamed of her poverty "act," but in her great egoism, she has probably convinced herself that Konstantine's ills are strictly form jealousy - of her success and of her lover - and not from any misaction on her part.

When Konstantine himself confronts his mother, the great tension of the play briefly explodes. The complexity of their relationship, consciously based on the Gertrude-Hamlet **theme**, is glimpsed in the violent flare-up. The tenderness between them, if not unnatural, is at least unusual. And yet they have never accepted each other. They are able to torment each other in an instant. In earlier versions of the play, Chekhov made much more explicit the Hamlet-Oedipus overtones of Konstantine's feelings for his mother, but the censor depleted these implications. Even without specific indications, we sense quite clearly that Konstantine is jealous of his mother's lover, jealous for affection he has never received. When he torments her with deprecations of her success and attacks her vanity, he is really crying out for her love and approval. When she annihilates him by screaming "nonentity" she is really protecting herself against his attacks and at the same time reasserting her control over him - a control she has exercised all his life.

Konstantine is reduced, much to his mother's triumphant satisfaction, to a helpless child once again. "I've lost everything," he weeps. "She [Nina] doesn't love me, now I can't write. All my hopes are gone." Ascendant once again, the mother consoles: "Don't despair. It will all pass. . . . She'll love you again."

The struggle for control repeats itself in part when Trigorin attempts to stay with Nina. Instead of bullying Trigorin, as she has her son, Arkadina flatters his virility and talent. "You are so talented, so intelligent, the best of all modern writers." And more than flattery, she exercises hysterical possession: "You are mine . . . you are mine. The brow is mine, and the eyes mine, and this beautiful silky hair, too, is mine." Detached and self-questioning, Trigorin was never meant to withstand such pressure. Like the child before him, Trigorin succumbs. "Take me, carry me away, only never let me be one step away from you."

A few moments later Arkadina foolishly does let him one step away, and in whispered **cliches** that are surely right out of his own novels, he accepts Nina's gift of herself.

ACT IV

Setting: One of the drawing rooms in Sorin's house, turned into a study by Konstantine. Books are stacked all about. It is evening. The sound from outside of trees rustling and the wind howling in the chimney.

Two years have passed, and Masha and Medvedenko have a baby whom Masha neglects in favor of staying at Sorin's where she can be near Konstantine. She abhors her husband and continues to pursue Konstantine, seeking the relationship her mother has with Dorn. Sorin is very ill, and Arkadina has been sent for. Dr. Dorn, who has been traveling in Europe, catches up on the news while he is away. He asks about Nina, and Konstantine tells him her story. She ran away from home and joined Trigorin. She had a child. The child died. Trigorin grew weary of her and returned to Arkadina. Nina toured the provinces as an actress and did very poorly. She is nervous and exhausted. She now plays in third-rate theaters and is plagued by the "attentions" of merchants.

Konstantine had followed her every move in the beginning but she would never see him. Afterwards, when he went back home, she wrote him letters, always signed "the seagull." For five days Nina has been staying at an inn in the town but she will not see anyone, and her parents have hired a watchman to keep her off their grounds.

Konstantine has had a minor success publishing stories in magazines. When Trigorin comes to Sorin's to join Arkadina, he brings the latest magazine with Konstantine's story in it. Trigorin says: "In Petersburg and in Moscow, everywhere, there's a great deal of interest in your work." But Konstantine notices that Trigorin has not even cut the pages of his story in the magazine.

Before dinner, on the evening Trigorin comes, a six-handed lotto game progresses. While the game goes on each character expresses his thoughts, none listening to the others and all pretending to be absorbed in the cards. Arkadina talks of the ovation she received at Kharkoff. Trigorin talks of Konstantine's style of writing: "there is something strange, vague, at times even like delirious raving. Not a single character that is alive." But he immediately relates Konstantine as writer to Trigorin as writer.

Sorin falls fast asleep. Dorn brings up his old point that Konstantine has talent: "It's only a pity that he's got no definite purpose. He creates impressions, never more than that." Arkadina tunes in long enough to say: "Imagine, I have not read him yet. There's never time." Shamreyeff, the orderly steward, brings up the seagull which Trigorin had long ago asked him to stuff but had never come back for. Trigorin cannot remember any seagull.

With the game finally ended everyone goes to dinner, leaving Konstantine in his study hard at work.

Though he has not succeeded, Konstantine has begun to see that "I've talked so much about new forms, but now I feel that little by little I am slipping into mere routine myself. . . . Yes, I'm coming more and more to the conclusion that it's a matter not of old forms and not of new forms, but that a man writes, not thinking at all of what forms to choose, writes because it comes pouring out from his soul."

As he muses, Nina sneaks in to visit him, making sure all the doors are locked against her discovery. She is overwrought, hysterical. She refers to herself as a seagull; she cries: "Life's brutal." Her last two years have been a devastating nightmare. Konstantine still adores her: "Ever since I lost you and began to get my work published my life has been unbearable... I'm miserable." Konstantine begs her to stay or take him with her. Nina is raving and frantic. But finally she controls herself and tells Konstantine in triumph: "I'm a real actress, I act with delight, with rapture. I'm drunk when I'm on the stage, and feel that I am beautiful... I have faith and when I think of my calling I'm not afraid of life."

Konstantine has no faith. He has not found his way. And Nina's triumph defeats him. As she leaves he can only lamely mutter: "Too bad if any one meets her in the garden and tells Mother. That might upset Mother."

The others return from dinner as Konstantine leaves the room, having torn up all his manuscripts. A few moments later a sound of a shot is heard offstage. Dorn goes to investigate, and while assuring everyone it was just some ether in his medicine bag which exploded; he takes Trigorin aside and says: "The fact is Konstantine Gavrilovich has shot himself."

Comment:

A serious play ending with the hero's death has every claim to tragedy. Why, then, did Chekhov specifically label *The Seagull* a comedy? It is surely not a comedy in the traditional sense of a drama which makes us laugh. The comedy in *The Seagull* is a comedy of posturing. We, through Chekhov's ironical psychological characterizing, perceive the tedium and insignificance of these people, who don't see their own triviality. Quite the opposite! They consider themselves important; but the audience sees the comic disparity between what they are and what they think they are.

Arkadina acts in popular, conventional plays in the provinces and is far from an important or even accomplished actress. She behaves as if she were an international star and we become so involved with her that we lose sight of her petty, boring existence, Konstantine hasn't even Arkadina's slight claim to fame. He is a confused and overwrought young man with very little talent. A country boy, he has pretensions of writing for the stage in brand-new forms -as so many sensitive young men from the provinces have dreamed of doing him. His foolish, almost adolescent, melancholic dramatizing over his failures culminate in his most extreme act of attention-seeking: suicide.

Konstantine's self-indulgence and self-pity are more neurotic and pathetic than tragic. And Chekhov's way of dramatizing his death makes his unimportance clear. In a tragedy, the hero dies onstage or his death is majestically described. Not only does Konstantine die offstage; no one even recognizes that a gun has gone off. And his death is reported quietly, so that Arkadina will not have a chance to play one of her insincere scenes.

In short, it is the vast disparity between the way these people talk about their lives and the way they actually live which makes the play a "comedy." In a later Chekhov play, *The Three Sisters*, a brooding character, Solyony, has played the role of a moody romantic hero for so long, despite his boring military life, that when he finally challenges the harmless young Baron Tusenbach to a duel he is firmly convinced that this is what he must do: he is playing a ludicrous role to its end. So with Konstantine. He has billed himself as the sensitive artist for so long, despite his lack of talent and industry, that suicide is the romantic conclusion to this failures.

Nina's fate, too, robs the play of its tragic aspects. She suffers real misery and despair and yet emerges with an optimistic and triumphant vision. She feels herself to be a real actress and with her soul growing "stronger every day" she has learned to "bear my cross and have faith." Nina's story does not evolve as the embodiment of the slain seagull. She is not utterly destroyed.

Chekhov's attempt at a new kind of drama is perfectly displayed in this act. A great deal happens to the characters, but we see none of it happen. Nina's entire sordid **episode** with Trigorin is revealed to us in a few short words. Masha's disastrous marriage and motherhood don't occur onstage. We don't see the main events in the characters' lives; Chekhov only dramatizes the psychological effect of these events on them as time passes and hope wanes.

The Seagull was Chekhov's first major attempt at a play of "indirect action" - a play in which truths about the psychological makeup of the characters were of greater concern than contrived actions for the sake of the dramatic. Chekhov was attempting a new kind of **realism**. Not realism of situation but **realism** of character. Given the characters and their environment, everything they say and do is wholly believable and natural. It is the situation itself which is not realistic in the conventional sense. The multiple love triangles, for instance, are highly improbable. How likely is it that in one household we would find: Shamreyeff-Dorn-Pauline; Masha-Konstantine-Nina; Konstantine-Nina-Trigorin; Nina-Trigorin-Arkadina; and potentially: Medvedenko-Marsha-Konstantine; and psychologically: Konstantine-Arkadina-Trigorin.

But given these triangles and accepting them as part of the dramatic situation, not one word or action is untrue to the life these people would live. Chekhov was experimenting with the depiction of "life as it is," not as dramatists had contrived it to be. And life "as it is" has very little external drama in it. That is why we only hear about Nina's tragedy, that is why Dorn says quietly and aside: "The fact is Konstantine Gavrilovich has shot himself." In life as it is, we don't witness suicides, we only hear about them and talk about them.

ANALYSIS OF SELECTED CHARACTERS

Arkadina

As a provincial actress of moderate repute, Mme. Arkadina is not really terribly important in the theater world. But in the setting of non-luminaries her importance is so exaggerated that she has become the center of a little universe. Arkadina is vain, selfish, grasping, and cruel. Her driving ambition, though not admirable, is the source of her triumphs. She does not doubt the greatness of her talent and art, and she marches unswervingly towards the goals she has in mind. That she destroys a son, tyrannizes a lover, and refuses to help a brother are of little moment to her. We do not learn why Arkadina behaves so selfishly -her past is never hinted at - but she is a devastating specimen of the neurotically destructive, yet somehow unfulfilled, middle-aged actress.

Konstantine

At twenty-five, Konstantine has had a full life of frustration. Made to mingle all his life with his mother's self-aggrandizing friends, he has always felt insignificant and worthless. In attempting to prove his worth he has written a foolish, childish, lifeless play. When his mother rejects his play and later his stories he is devastated. The prime force in Konstantine's life is his mother. His attachment to her is still that of the dependent child, an attachment she does nothing to discourage. Her approval and acceptance of him motivates all his actions, and when she rejects him he turns to Nina in her place. When Nina, too, spurns him he is left, as it were, motherless, helpless, and moribund. Konstantine is the prototype of the sensitive, not very talented, misunderstood youth.

Nina

A the outset, Nina is a young, stage-struck impressionable provincial. She is graceful and charming and wholly dazzled by the grandeur she thinks she finds at Sorin's. When she falls in love with Trigorin she is primarily falling in love with his fame and success and only later, after she has found herself as an actress, does she love him maturely. Nina's great suffering does not destroy her; she emerges from it with faith and dedication, making her the only positive character in the play.

Trigorin

A famous and successful writer, Trigorin is wholly detached from the life around him. His preoccupation with his work makes him negligent and flexible about everything else. He pays no attention to his clothes, is willing to accede to Arkadina's wish to take him away from Nina, forgets about Nina as soon as he is through with her. And yet Trigorin is likeable. He is honest about himself and his abilities, he is gracious about his success, and he is willing to live and let live. He did not ruin Nina out of malice. He loved her briefly and when he was bored he left. He probably expected her to do the same and would have been shocked to see her so devastated as a result of their affair. Trigorin is a competent craftsman obsessed with his craft - an unpretentious and engaging man with the best of intentions.

ESSAY QUESTION AND ANSWER

Question: How is the seagull used as a symbol in the play?

Answer: Chekhov has woven the symbol of the seagull into the very fiber of the play. It does not stand as an isolated and nonfunctional abstraction, but rather applies to the entire setting and to the characters individually. As part of the atmosphere, the seagull represents beauty, freedom, and integrity to which the characters are drawn but which they kill through their pettiness and selfishness. Each of the characters on Sorin's estate is seeking some truth, some freedom, but each (except Nina) is thwarted in his search by the very structure of his life and the grossness of those around him.

The major characters are summarized in their relation to the slain bird in a much more specific way than the general search for beauty and truth. For Trigorin, life has meaning only as it is functional for his novels. He does not enjoy life but removes himself from it in order to use it. Thus for him the beautiful bird is an idea for a story. Alive, the bird had no meaning for him. Shot and stuffed it is an inspiration. He handles life the same way. The viable and moving must be shot and stuffed, captured and killed to provide copy. Once it is used for his obsessive ends it is forgotten. Just as he forgets about the stuffed gull, so he forgets about Nina.

Konstantine sees the wantonly destroyed bird as an embodiment of himself. Like the gull, he envisions himself as a free and beautiful creature at one with nature. The selfishness of man destroyed the bird (Konstantine himself killed it out of idleness), and the selfishness of man leads to Konstantine's destruction. Probably the same gun which killed the seagull killed Konstantine. Such a symbolic act would be true to Konstantine's conscious identification with beauty as well as his flair for the dramatic.

Nina, too, identifies with the bird, so much so that in her hysteria at the end she repeats over and over: "I am a seagull." The story that Trigorin fashions from the dead bird becomes Nina's story. But Nina's life goes beyond his little tale. She survives her destruction with the strength, will, and dedication necessary to great art. She was the seagull but is no more.

As for Arkadina, the true destructive force in the play, she never knows of the seagull. She assists in the death of all that it stands for in general, but blinded by her vanity, selfishness, and ambition she would never perceive the bird, dead or alive.

The seagull is not an isolated emblem. A whole pyramid of symbols support it: the lake, the estate the state used for Konstantine's play, the relationship of the minor characters. But it is the poetic and dramatic center around which the play revolves.

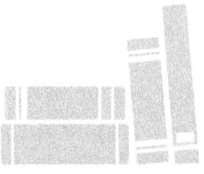

UNCLE VANYA

INTRODUCTION

Nobody is quite clear about the date of composition of *Uncle Vanya*. In December, 1896, Chekhov wrote to his friend Suvorin about *"Uncle Vanya*, which is not known to anyone in the world." And in a letter to Maxim Gorky dated December 3, 1898, he says: *"Uncle Vanya* was written long ago." At any rate, Vanya first appeared in print in a collection of Chekhov's works published in 1897. The play was immediately picked up by numerous provincial theaters, which performed it with great success.

Moscow audiences did not see *Vanya* for two years after it was published. At first, because he had always wanted a play staged at a large, important theater, Chekhov offered *Vanya* to an imperial theater, and not the Moscow Art Theater, which had scored such a triumph with *The Seagull*. The Art Theater's fabled director, Stanislavsky, describes what happened during the negotiations with the imperial theater.

"Chekhov was handed a report from the Repertoire Committee of the theater in which there were many flattering words about his play, which it accepted for production in the theater, on one condition, however - that the author change the end of the third act, in which the indignant Uncle Vanya shoots Professor Serebriakoff.

"It is impossible to think," read the report, "that an enlightened, cultured man like Uncle Vanya could shoot on the stage at a person with a diploma, that is, Professor Serebriakoff."

Chekhov reddened with indignation at the foolishness of the report and at once broke out into prolonged and happy laughter when he quoted the above sentence. . . ."

What probably amused Chekhov was that on the selection committee of the theater sat several professors, who doubtless were highly affronted by the playwright's rough handling of the egotistical Professor Serebriakoff.

Uncle Vanya finally went to its rightful theater, the Moscow Art Theater. The play opened in Moscow on October 26, 1899, to a mixed reception. But as both performers and audiences began to understand the **realism** raised to the level of symbol, and as Chekhov's new dramatic method, experimented with in *The Seagull* and refined in *Vanya* grew to be accepted, the play became a smashing success.

Uncle Vanya had a curious history. In 1889, Chekhov submitted a play called *The Wood Demon* to the Petersburg Dramatic and Literary Committee. The Committee rejected the play as being nothing more than "a dramatized short story." Producers in both Moscow and Petersburg found the play unfit for the stage. After much revision, *The Wood Demon* was finally put on in December of 1889. It was a miserable failure. The play teemed with coincidences, melodramatic devices, and superfluous subplots. After attempting further revisions, Chekhov ultimately abandoned the play.

It was *The Wood Demon*, pruned down, tightened, with a new pivotal situation and minus several characters, which emerged as *Uncle Vanya* in the collected works of 1897. Many of the scenes and much of the dialogue have been retained in *Vanya*, but Chekhov considered it an entirely new play, and in 1900 when he was asked for permission to produce *The Wood Demon* Chekhov said he hated the play and wanted to forget he had ever written it.

Although Vanya was written around the same time as *The Seagull*, its dramatic intensity and psychological truth allies it with the perfected plays of a later date.

CHARACTERS

Alexander Serebriakoff

An elderly, retired professor, widowed and remarried to a young woman. Serebriakoff lives on the estate managed by his first wife's brother.

Elena Serebriakoff

The twenty-seven-year-old second wife of the old professor. She is beautiful, captivating, selfish.

Ivan Voinitskaya (Uncles Vanya)

Brother of Serebriakoff's first wife. Vanya is forty-seven and in love with Elena.

Sofia Serebriakoff (Sonia)

Serebriakoff's daughter by his first marriage, in love with Dr. Astroff. She lives with her Uncle Vanya.

Mikhail Astroff

A provincial doctor, overworked and embittered by his isolated existence.

Maria Voinitskaya

Mother of Uncle Vanya and the professor's first wife. A foolish old woman who dotes on the professor's every word.

Ilya Telegin

An impoverished landowner living on the estate. Nicknamed "Waffles" because of his pockmarked skin.

Marina

An old nurse.

ACT I

Setting: A garden of an estate. A table is set for tea. It is past two in the afternoon of a cloudy day.

Professor Alexander Serebriakoff has retired, after twenty-five years, from University work. From lack of funds he has left town and gone to live on the estate owned by his first wife's family. His first wife, Vera Petrovna, has been dead for almost ten years and the professor, late in life, has married a young and beautiful woman, Elena. The daughter of his first marriage, Sonia, lives on the estate with her mother's brother, Uncle Vanya, and her grandmother. Together, Sonia and Vanya have worked mightily to keep the estate flourishing. Vanya's mother (Sonia's grandmother), Maria Voinitskaya, is a great fan of Serebriakoff and follows closely all the articles and pamphlets he publishes.

Since Serebriakoff and Elena have come to live on the estate, life has been topsy-turvy. Pretending to be highly absorbed in writing his pretentious and worthless articles, Serebriakoff has shattered the established routine of the household. Dinner is served when he is ready, the tea grows cold in the samovar awaiting his descent from his study.

Vanya, who was once a great admirer of Serebriakoff's intellect, has finally opened his eyes to the professor's worthlessness. In a passionately bitter speech Vanya pretends to compose Serebriakoff's biography: "A retired professor... an old crust, a learned old dried mackerel. Gout, rheumatism, migraine, and his liver swollen with jealousy and envy.... Forever complains of his misfortunes, though as a matter of fact, he is unusually lucky.... A man for exactly twenty-five years reads and writes about art, and understands exactly nothing about art.... Twenty-five years reads and writes about what intelligent people already know and stupid people are not interested in.... He retired, and he is not known to a single living soul, he is absolutely unknown. ... But, mind you, he strides about like a demigod."

Vanya is not only bitter about Serebriakoff's pretensions and worthlessness, but he is envious of his success with women. At forty-seven, Vanya has spent a reclusive life toiling on the estate, while the dried mackerel married first Vanya's gentle, beautiful sister and now the ravishing Elena.

Elena, like her husband, is a great egotist. Although she has sacrificed her youth and beauty to marry a famous man, she does not welcome overtures from younger men. Vanya, at the end of the act, captivated by her beauty, declares his love for her. Elena cruelly shuts him off: "Thanks to you, soon there will be no faithfulness, no purity, no capacity for sacrifice left on earth. Why can't you look at a woman with indifference if she is not yours? Because . . . in all of you sits the demon of destruction."

The night before the play opens, Serebriakoff has had another attack of his rheumatism or gout. The family doctor, Astroff, has been summoned. When he arrives, Serebriakoff seems to have recovered, or at any rate will not see the doctor.

As a provincial medical man, Astroff has not "had one free day" in ten years. He is ceaselessly called out day and night to attend peasants, factory workers, laborers. Astroff has grown numb from his overwork: "There's nothing I want, nothing I need, nobody I love." The only thing that stirs the doctor is his love of trees. His passion is to preserve the woods for nature's purposes and for beauty. To Astroff the destruction of trees is the destruction of life: "Man is endowed with intellect and creative powers so that he may multiply what is given to him, but up to now he has not created but destroyed."

Young Sonia, Serebriakoff's daughter, is overwhelmed by Astroff's intellect and dedication. She has fallen in love with the doctor, but although he has spent a great deal of time over the years at the estate, he does not appear to return Sonia's interest.

Vanya and Sonia not only support on the estate Serebriakoff and Elena, who have been there just a few months, but a few others as well: Vanya's mother, who dotes on her son-in-law's published words; Telegin, a bankrupt neighbor (called "Waffles" because of his pock-marked face); and an old nurse, Marina.

There are only two actions in the act. Astroff is called away to tend to a factory worker and Vanya declares his love for Elena. For the rest, the act is an introduction to the characters and their leitmotifs.

Comment:

Literally nothing happens in the way of direct action that has not happened countless times before on Vanya's estate. But the tensions and character "themes" are dramatically and subtly exposed.

The only piece of overt action relevant to the play, Vanya's desperate declaration of love, has clearly been made before. Elena protests, as she probably has often before: "Don't look at me that way, I don't like it." And Vanya pleads: "How can I look at you differently if I love you?" Obviously, this is not the first time he has made the plea.

If for the characters the conversations and exchanges are hackneyed and repetitious, for the audience they set up dramatic and dangerous conflicts. Vanya's entrance, surely unique for a play of the 1890s, gives us a hint of the havoc to come. For a leading character's first entrance, the stage direction is revolutionary:

"Voinitsky comes out of the house; he has had a nap after lunch and looks rumpled. He sits down on the bench as he arranges his stylish necktie." Vanya's first line is: "Yes . . . (a pause) Yes. . . ." These two "yeses" are filled with meaning. Vanya has seen through his own mistaken life. "Up to last year, I deliberately tried . . . to blind my eyes with pedantry . . . and not to see real life - and I thought I was doing well. And now, if you only knew! I don't sleep nights because of disappointment, and anger that I so stupidly let time slip by." The two affirmatives are meant to convey all that he understands about his own wasted life.

Stanislavsky, the director who first staged *Uncle Vanya*, tells of the difficulty he and his company had in understanding Vanya. At first they accepted "that Uncle Vanya is a member of the landed gentry who manages the estate of the old Professor Serebriakoff. The costume and the general appearance of a landed gentleman are known to all, high boots, a cap, sometimes a horsewhip, for it is taken for granted that he rides horseback a great deal."

When Chekhov attended rehearsals he was furious at this interpretation. "Listen," he said, "he has a wonderful tie; he is an elegant, cultured man. It is not true that our landed gentry walk about in boots smeared with tar. They are wonderful people. They dress well. They order their clothes in Paris." Stanislavsky suddenly understood the play and "from that time on, Uncle Vanya became for us a cultured, soft, elegant, poetic, fine type of man."

What has happened to Vanya is that for years he was blinded by Serebriakoff's reputed brilliance. On the basis of rumors from Petersburg, Vanya had worked and doted in the darkest corner of the provinces, thriving on the supposed fame and brilliance of his brother-in-law. But Vanya, the truly gifted, intelligent, and sensitive one, has now, too late, seen through the phony, foolish professor whom he must now support.

It is important to remember that Vanya is a true gentleman: intelligent, honest, and elegant. And that the years he has spent in misguided isolation have made him bitter and cynical - but in no wise foolish or ungracious.

This great disappointment, rooted in his sudden exposure of Serebriakoff, is Vanya's "leitmotif." Other characters have other themes. Vanya's mother, a garrulous old fool, reads Serebriakoff's works like a Bible. She remains blinded to his arid intellectuality and thrives on his every word, even though "he disapproves of what seven years ago he himself defended."

Astroff has two themes: his own exhaustion and waste; and the beauty and understanding to be gained from the preservation of nature. Like Vanya, Astroff is a brilliant and gentle scholar condemned to the provinces. His passion for forestry ("Forests are fewer and fewer, rivers dry up, game becomes extinct, the climate is ruined, and every day the earth gets poorer and uglier") is not meant to be ridiculous at all. Chekhov himself was a vociferous advocate of natural preservation.

The tension and malaise on the estate is reaching an intolerable peak. Elena is tired of people pitying her sacrifice and attempting to disillusion her about her old fool of a husband. Marina, the old nurse, is frantic about the household's disrupted routine. Sonia, who secretly loves Astroff, is fighting a losing battle in her attempts to placate the antagonists. Only the egomaniacal Serebriakoff and his stubborn mother-in-law follow their old routines, oblivious to the tension which is mounting around them.

ACT II

Setting: A dining room in Serebriakoff's house. It is night. A storm is brewing.

No one has slept in the household for two or three nights. Serebriakoff, with pains in his legs and difficulty in breathing, has demanded a constant vigil. Past midnight, Elena is sitting with her husband, who is cantankerous and self-pitying. In a burst of indignation, Serebriakoff accuses Elena of finding it "revolting to look at me." "This damned, disgusting old age, the devil take it!" he grumbles. Elena's patience is thin: "You speak of your old age as if we were all guilty of your being old."

Serebriakoff accuses the entire household of impatiently awaiting his death and becoming tired of him, and he is offended: "Well, let us suppose I am revolting, I am an egotist, I am a despot - but don't I really, even in my old age, have some right to egotism? As if I have not earned it? As if . . . I have no right to a quiet old age, to some attention from people?" Serebriakoff complains about being stuck in this "morgue," listening to stupid conversations when he could be with his "esteemed colleagues." "I want to live, I love success, I love fame, applause and . . . here I am like an exile."

When Vanya comes to relieve Elena at the vigil, Serebriakoff rudely throws him out, yelling: "He'll talk my head off." Finally old Marina comes in and offers tender sympathy: "Does it hurt? . . . This is your old ailment . . . Dear sir, let's go to bed."

Elena, left alone with Vanya, recounts the evils which beset the household. "Your mother hates everything except her pamphlets and the professor; the professor is cross, he won't trust me, and is afraid of you; Sonia is angry at her father, she is angry at me and hasn't spoken to me for two weeks now; you hate my husband and openly scorn your mother; I'm irritable.... Things are not going very well in this house."

Vanya is overcome with his sense of frustration and waste. "Day and night like a fiend at my throat is the thought that my life is hopelessly lost.... This feeling of mine is dying in vain, like a ray of sunlight that has strayed into a pit."

Vanya has been drinking with Astroff, and again he pleads with Elena for her love. She is harsh with him. "Go to bed! I am bored with you."

She leaves, and in a touching soliloquy, Vanya tells how he has wasted his life. "I adored the professor, that pitiful, gouty creature, I worked for him like ox!" For years Sonia and Vanya had lived like "thrifty peasants," often going hungry themselves so that they could get together enough money to send to the professor. Vanay used to "Live and breathe" his pride in his relative's learning and fame. But Vanya has learned: "He is absolutely unknown, he is nothing! A soap bubble! And I've been fooled."

Sonia, who still toils on the farm, serves as a constant reminder of how he has misspent his life and how slothful he has become.

When Sonia and Astroff are alone for a moment Astroff confesses to the young girl that he is charmed by Elena's beauty, while recognizing her selfishness and lack of delicate soul. For Astroff there is no longer any "little light in the distance" toward which he can move during his hard days. He is defeated by stupid people and the monotony of his life.

Sonia, infatuated by his intensity and ceaseless work, flatters him: "You are refined, you have such a gentle voice . . . more than that you are . . . like nobody else - you are beautiful." In her enthusiasm, Sonia gets Astroff to promise he will stop drinking.

Later, when Sonia and Elena are alone, they patch up their quarrel of two weeks' standing and Elena tells Sonia why she married her father: "I married him for love. I was infatuated with him as a learned and famous man. My love was not real; my love was artificial, but it seemed real to me then."

The two women suddenly become intimate and discuss Elena's unhappiness and the doctor's great bravery, free mind, and genius. Excited, Elena says she would like to play the piano, which she has not touched for a long time. "I shall play and cry - cry like a fool." Sonia goes to ask her father if Elena might play without disturbing him. She returns with his message: "No, you cannot!"

Comment:

As in so many of Chekhov's plays, this second act moves forward in a series of two-by-two interviews. Throughout the evening, people are coming and going, and as they pass each other they share confidences and exchange or reveal information.

The first interview, between Serebriakoff and Elena, shows us just how cantankerous and egocentric the old professor really is and how tiresome is Elena's life with him. It also shows us that Elena is not pulling off her much-touted self-sacrifice with any great success -she is almost as selfish as her fraudulent husband. Serebriakoff's selfishness and self-pity are monumental. He takes no cognizance of the sacrifices which have been made in his behalf - he only knows that he is being deprived of the public acclaim which has sustained him for twenty-five years, and that he is growing old. He has no perspective on his own worthlessness.

The brief exchange between Vanya and the professor is bitterly ironic. Vanya has seen through Serebriakoff's pretensions, and yet it is the professor who abjures Vanya's company because he talks too much.

In the interview Vanya and Elena we learn directly of Elena's "rhetoric, her idle moralizing, her foolish, idle thoughts about the end of the world." And we hear from Vanya how total his defeat is. "No past, it was stupidly spent on trifles, and the present with all its absurdity is frightful." Elena cruelly rejects Vanya's love declarations; his intensity of feeling only leaves her "numb." The passion that Elena's rejection arouses, drives Vanya to a bitter soliloquy when she leaves.

From Vanya we learn of his huge and worthless sacrifice. He has devoted all his youth and energy to a great principle - the professor's search for knowledge and truth. And now, exhausted and spent with the effort, he discovers the search was a useless fraud. For a "soap bubble" he has worn himself out with manual labor in an isolated province. The only passion left him is his love for the scornful Elena.

Astroff interrupts Vanya's bitter soliloquy. Between the two old friends there is a clear sense of intimacy and sympathy. Astroff, when he is drunk, can still believe "that I am bringing an enormous boon to humanity." Vanya has no such comfort. And in his interview with Sonia we see how little is left to him. "Everything is rotting" on the farm, she accuses, "and you occupy yourself with illusions. You have neglected ohe farming completely." Vanya's inertia and defeat spread even to the land he has labored all his life to cultivate.

Between Sonia and Astroff there is a long and many-leveled exchange. Sonia, with heart in mouth, is trying to convey her love and admiration to Astroff. The doctor is using Sonia as a sounding board for the broad spectrum of his discontent. He talks of Elena's beauty, which "charms us all" - this to the homely Sonia, of whom people say "she is kind, generous, but it's a pity she is not pretty." He speaks of his contempt for rural Russian life, of his own fatigue, of the shallowness of the intelligentsia, and of his own inability to love. And finally, he confesses: "What still enthralls me is beauty. . . . It seems to me that if Elena . . . only wanted to, in one day she could set my head in a whirl."

The final interview, between Elena and Sonia, reveals Elena's calculating motives for marriage and her admiration for Astroff's "genius" and sacrifice.

In terms of direct action next to nothing has happened. The professor was sleepless with his various aches and pains, Astroff and Vanya have been drinking, and Vanya has once more declared his love for Elena. And yet the drama and tension have vastly heightened.

The startling news that for twenty-five years Vanya has sacrificed his life to support the vainglorious professor painfully intensifies his utter defeat. He not only despises Serebriakoff's emptiness, but he has devoted his youth to it. The hint that Astroff is attracted to Elena sets up the emotional tangle of Vanya-Elena-Astroff; Sonia-Astroff-Elena; Astroff-Elena-Serebriakoff. The professor's hatred of rural life vastly complicates his relationship to the household. He is an unwanted guest, or more correctly, parasite, who despises the hospitality he is offered.

In the first act we glimpsed the household's state of decay. In the second act we see for ourselves the totality of the moral and physical collapse.

ACT III

Setting: Living room in Serebriakoff's estate. It is the middle of the day.

Various members of the household are waiting in the living room for Serebriakoff. The professor has asked everyone to gather at one o'clock for an important piece of business. While they wait, Sonia, Elena, and Vanya bicker. The tension has clearly mounted. Vanya snipes at Elena: 'She walks around and sways a bit from laziness. Very sweet Very!" Elena cries out: "I am dying of boredom, I don't know what to do." Sonia admonishes: "Occupy yourself with running the house, teaching the children, caring for the sick."

Elena's boredom has become infectious. Uncle Vanya no longer does any work on the estate and he follows Elena around like a shadow. Sonia is ready to drop work at any time of day.

Astroff has forsaken both his woods and his medicine and hangs around the Serebriakoff's every day.

After cruel words, Vanya offers to bring a bouquet of roses as a peace offering to Elena. He leaves to fetch the flowers. Left alone, Sonia and Elena talk of Astroff: "I have loved him now for six years. . . . He is here every day now but does not look at me, doesn't see me," moans Sonia. Elena offers to talk to Astroff and find out whether or not he loves Sonia. If he does not, Elena will tell him to stop coming to the house.

In a soliloquy, Elena herself plays with the idea of giving in to "the charms of such a man." It is tempting "to fly away like a free bird. Away from you all, from your sleepy faces, from your conversations, to forget that you exist in the world." But Elena knows herself to be too cowardly and convention-bound-she will never fly.

When Astroff comes in, he shows the disinterested Elena the charts he has been keeping on the destruction of the natural resources of the district. "We have here a case of degeneration that results from a struggle that's beyond men's strength for existence; degeneration caused by sloth, by ignorance, by the complete absence of any conscience."

Elena interrupts him with her cross-examination about Sonia. Astroff admits that he respects Sonia but does not like her as a woman. He agrees to stop coming to the house if his presence makes Sonia unhappy. Suddenly Astroff moves close to Elena: "You darling bird of prey, don't look at me like that. I am a wise old sparrow. . . . A beautiful, fluffy little thing . . . you must have victims!" Astroff heatedly proposes that Elena meet him in the forest the next day. She struggles and protests. Finally Astroff kisses her. Elena reluctantly resists him. Just then Vanya returns with his bouquet for Elena. Caught in the act and greatly embarrassed, Astroff edges out. Elena, in a frenzy, begs Vanya to help her and Serebriakoff to leave the estate that very day.

Just then Serebriakoff comes in with the rest of the household. Sonia quickly goes to Elena and asks impatiently: "What did he say? . . . He said that he will not be here anymore . . . yes?" And Elena nods her head.

Serebriakoff proceeds with the business for which he has called them together: "The fact is . . . I am old, sick, and therefore find it timely to regulate my property terms. . . . To go on living in the country is impossible for me. Yet to live in town on the income we get from this estate is impossible. . . . Our estate gives an average of not more than two percent. I propose to sell it. If the proceeds we convert into interest-bearing paper, then we will receive from four to five percent, and I think there will even be a surplus of several thousand, which will allow us to buy a small villa in Finland."

Vanya's first reaction to the impossible proposal is incredulity. "And where would you order me to go with my old mother and with Sonia here?" Then comes the anger: "Up to now I was so stupid as to think that this estate belongs to Sonia." Vanya is so furious he is almost speechless and Serebriakoff immediately backs down: "I don't say my project is ideal. If everybody finds it unsuitable then I will not insist."

Vanya is not to be mollified: "This estate would not have been bought had I not given up my inheritance in favor of my sister. . . . As if that were not enough, for ten years I worked like an ox, and paid off the entire debt. . . . For twenty-five years I have managed this estate, worked, sent you money, like a most conscientious clerk, and during all that time you not once thanked me. All the time - both in my youth and now - you paid me five hundred roubles a year for wages - fit for a beggar - and never once thought of increasing it by even one rouble!" Serebriakoff is stunned and indignant at the outburst. He prepares to leave in a righteous huff, but Vanya bars his way. "You have ruined my life! I have not lived, I have not lived! . . . You are my worst enemy!"

Finally Vanya dashes into another room warning Serebriakoff: "You will remember me!"

Elena convinces her husband to make peace and the two of them go after Vanya. Suddenly there is a shot off stage. Serebriakoff runs in, panicked, followed by Vanya holding a revolver. Vanya takes aim and fires at the professor again - and again misses. Exhausted, he drops the revolver and murmurs in despair: "Oh, what am I doing! What am I doing."

Comment:

Although the audible and visible pistol shots appear to be the **climax** of the play, at least in terms of direct action, we must keep in mind that Chekhov was not writing a traditional drama of action. The actual turning point of the indirect action, of the psychological unveiling of the characters, comes in Vanya's outburst before the shooting. Suddenly Vanya realizes that everything he had feared about the futility of his life, all he had bemoaned, was in fact true. He really had sacrificed his life for the old goat of a professor; his life really is as meaningless and worthless as he had been saying it was for a year.

Vanya's desperation and venom are well founded. He has just seen the woman he loves (and who has spurned him) in the arms of another admirer. He knows that his beloved niece is hopelessly in love with the same man and is being made bitterly unhappy by his lack of attention. He is frantic with his own sloth and inactivity. From the vigorous farm manager he has become a shadow trailing in Elena's path. But most of all, Vanya is desperate about the deception which governed his life. "For twenty-five years with this mother here I sat like a mole inside these four walls. . . . You were to us a creature of the highest order and your articles we knew by heart. . . . All your works, that I used to love, are not worth a brass penny! You fooled us!"

The literary committee of a Moscow Repertoire Company found it "impossible to think that an enlightened, cultured man like Uncle Vanya could shoot on the stage at a person with a diploma." But at the moment of the shooting, Vanya has lost all his enlightenment and culture, has lost the meaning of his life, and nothing is more plausible than that he should shoot at the cause of his torment.

In *The Wood Demon*, the precursor to *Uncle Vanya*, Chekhov had Vanya shoot himself after the argument with Serebriakoff. But that suicide was a sign of the undeveloped dramatist. As the critic Eric Bentley points out: "In the earlier version the fates of the characters are settled; in the later they are unsettled. In the earlier version they are settled, moreover, not by their own nature or by force of circumstance, but by theatrical **convention**. In the later their fate is unsettled because that is Chekhov's view of truth." To have Vanya kill himself is a pat, dramatic, but untruthful solution. To have him fire at and miss Serebriakoff solves no dramatic problems, but portrays life as it is.

The scene between Elena and Astroff was also absent from *The Wood Demon*. Since Chekhov, in the early version, was attempting to establish the mood of comedy with a happy ending, Astroff ends up in love with Sonia, not infatuated with Elena. Astroff here does not love Elena. He is fascinated by her beauty, just as, before she came, he was fascinated with the beauty of his forests. For Elena, he has deserted his trees. "Here I am already a whole month not doing anything, I have dropped everything, I look greedily for you."

Serebriakoff's proposal to sell the estate is so selfish and thoughtless as to be almost comic. He has probably never given a thought to Vanya's sacrifices in the past nor to his provisions for the future. He only knows: "What I cannot digest is the regime of country life. I have a feeling as if I had fallen from the earth on to some foreign planet."

The professor is genuinely surprised at Vanya's vehement reaction to his proposal. It had never occurred to him that Vanya had any attachment to the estate nor did he ever give thought one way or the other to the minute salary he had been paying Vanya. In short, Serebriakoff has never paid the slightest attention to anything which did not immediately concern himself - he is a caricature of the worthless egocentric.

The actions in this act of both Uncle Vanya and Dr. Astroff are central to the understanding of the extent of their deterioration. Both are (or have been) cultured, refined, idealistic gentlemen. Both have been confined in the dreary provinces and both have been chained to a life of drudgery. As a young man, Astroff would never have hungrily chased a selfish, destructive, and vain woman - a woman already married. And a year ago, the gentle and sacrificing Vanya would have been incapable of firing the revolver (although his bad aim at such close range shows that he is yet not a murderer). The life of boredom and frustration, the revelation of mistaken dreams has transformed both men - and the extent to which it has transformed them is the measure of its oppressiveness.

ACT IV

Setting: Vanya's bedroom-office. Papers, bookcases, scales are all about. There is a birdcage with a starling. On the wall a map of Africa, which apparently is of no use to anyone here. It is an autumn evening; all is tranquil.

Elena and Serebriakoff are leaving momentarily for Kharkov. They are in such a hurry they are not even taking their luggage. Telegin has hidden Vanya's revolver in the cellar lest he do further damage. But Vanya has thought of another means of self-destruction -he has stolen a jar of morphine from Astroff's medicine bag. Astroff, with reasoning and pleas, cannot get Vanya to tell where he has hidden the jar. When Sonia comes in she appeals to her uncle's courage: "Give it back, Uncle Vanya! I am just as unhappy as you are, maybe, but I don't despair. I bear it and I will bear it till the end of my life. Then you bear it too."

Vanya relents and returns the morphine, begging Sonia that they get to work immediately or he cannot survive. When Vanya goes to make his peace with Serebriakoff, Elena and Astroff are left alone. Astroff makes one last appeal that Elena come with him to the forest, but both of them know it is out of the question.

As they part, Astroff muses: "It is odd somehow . . . we have known each other, and suddenly for some reason - we will never see each other again. And that's how it is in this world." On an impulse they embrace and then it is finished.

Vanya and Serebriakoff have smoothed over their quarrel and Vanya assures the professor: "You will receive what you used to receive accurately. Everything will be as always."

The Serebriakoff's leave and Sonia and Vanya settle down to work. Vanya's mother sits down with her pamphlets and Marina takes up her knitting. Only Astroff fidgets. He has called for his carriage but he is reluctant to leave. He thanks Vanya for his hospitality, he takes a drink of vodka (his promise to Sonia to stop drinking is forgotten), he talks of one of his horses who is lame, he fusses over the map of Africa. But finally, when his carriage is ready, he leaves, with Sonia holding a light for him.

Sonia returns and sits down next to Vanya at the work table. Telegin comes in and gently strums his guitar. Marina yawns over her knitting. Vanya's mother makes notes in the margins of her pamphlets. The bells of Astroff's departing carriage are heard in the distance. In the old, familiar setting the overwrought and exhausted young Sonia delivers one of the most moving speeches in all of Chekhov's plays. She assures Vanya that one day, when all their work is over, they will peacefully rest.

Comment:

In an effort to make attractive generalizations about Chekhov's plays, critics often suggest that all the major works center about the changes effected by a newcomer's arrival on an established scene. This is true for some of the plays. It is not true for *Vanya*. Granted that the direct action (what there is of it) stems from the Serebriakoffs' visit, the indirect action, the characters' states of mind, change not at all.

Chekhov is at great pains to show that the old life will continue exactly as before. Marina delights that "We'll live again, the way it used to be in the old days . . . everything in its proper order." Vanya assures Serebriakoff that everything will be as always; Astroff will return "not before summer very likely," visiting only when someone is ill; and life on the estate, in the final scene, is exactly as it always was.

What has happened during the play is recognition. Those characters capable of it have recognized that their life is exactly what they had thought it to be, and no miracle is going to change it. Vanya, Astroff, Sonia, and Elena have come to accept, with resignation, the facts of their existence. They have determined with full reason what their lives are about and they will not be tempted again by the false hope that things will change. The unthinking characters - Marina, Telegin, old Maria Vasilievna, and the gouty professor - return to the old order with no recognition. They are glad to have everything in its place again, and the brief interruption was merely an inconvenience not a revelation.

The whole of this last act is a preparation for the final "composition" on which the curtain falls. And what a composition that is! The sounds are of Vanya's clicking abacus, Astroff's departing bells, Telegin's soft guitar, the tapping of the night watchman outside, closing everyone safely in. The physical movement is Marina knitting, Maria Vasilievna writing in her pamphlets, Vanya stroking Sonia's hair, Sonia wiping away tears. And the words are of a "long line of days, endless evenings" that shall someday end in rest.

The sense of tragedy is so heavy in this final scene that we forget no one has died, no one is maimed, nothing has happened to these people. Their great tragedy is the death of their dreams (which they never had reason to believe in) and their resignation to a life of futility.

ANALYSIS OF SELECTED CHARACTERS

Vanya

At forty-seven, Uncle Vanya is a prototype of the Russian gentleman, cultured, refined, and gentle, wasting his life in the provinces. Aside from Astroff there is not a kindred soul anywhere in the neighborhood. He has, perhaps foolishly, devoted his entire life to an ideal, and when that ideal turns out to be a "soap bubble" he is annihilated. Vanya, as his name in

Russian implies, is a lovable character. Uncle Vanya's English equivalent is "Uncle Johnny." The name immediately calls up affection and warm childhood feelings. Vanya is meant to be loved and we are meant to have good feeling for him. This makes his horrendous discovery of his own deception all the more moving and sorrowful.

Astroff

The doctor is nearly ten years younger than Vanya, and he seems to be of a hardier breed. He admits he is fascinated by Elena's beauty and that's all, while Vanya protests his love for the whole woman. Astroff at the outset works like a man obsessed. By the end he dissipates himself with the same vigor. Astroff, being emotionally removed from the state of affairs on the estate, is naturally more objective about them. His life has been empty, much as Vanya's has. Although he has slaved at his practice and his forests, somehow his devotion to them must have been shallow, for he turns both over in a twinkling to be around Elena.

Elena

As a young and beautiful woman, Elena creates in the play a fascinating center of destruction. She has married the old professor, not from love but from infatuation with his fame and "learning." Elena is lazy and selfish. She is wasting her life, but she finds it uninteresting to "teach and cure sick peasants." She has no purpose or goal in life; she is "merely a passing face." Just as she can no longer bear her life with the cantankerous professor, neither has she the energy nor the initiative to flee. Elena is intelligent and capable, but she is wasting her life in idleness.

Sonia

Sonia embodies the positive forces in the play struggling to stave off the incursion of evil. She is idealistic, pure, and energetic. Where Elena is beautiful, Sonia is homely. Where Elena is selfish and lazy, Sonia is thoughtful and hard-working. Elena has the ability to fascinate, Sonia has the qualities to be loved. Neither triumphs.

ESSAY QUESTIONS AND ANSWERS

Question: In light of Sonia's final speech, do you think Chekhov is offering "work" as the solution to the ills on the Serebriakoff estate?

Answer: Sonia's closing speech is the solution found by an overwrought young girl, not by Chekhov. If Chekhov were suggesting that these provincial problems could be solved, by work or any other means, he would be going against the principles of his own dramatic method - to show life as it really is, with no solutions, no melodramas.

Hard work is far from touted in the play. Astroff, who has not had one free day in ten years, is strangled by his "boring, stupid, dirty" life. His ceaseless efforts, with no time for himself, have left him broken, bored and growing "odd." Astroff has devoted himself to humanity, and yet his never-ending work, even with an ideal at the end, has broken him.

Vanya, too, has toiled all his life. Even before he discovered his labors were for a "soap bubble" he was bored, frustrated, and loveless. In showing how devastating hard work is when performed for a real or mistaken ideal, Chekhov surely cannot be suggesting that work in and of itself is any solution.

After all, Serebriakoff has worked too. He too has devoted himself to great principles-knowledge and education. Unlike Vanya he never discovers how mistaken his devotion is, and how inept he is at performing it, and yet, with clear and idealistic goals in view, the professor is the meanest, poorest example of mankind in the lot.

In three separate examples, Chekhov shows us that a life of labor is no answer to life's problems. Sonia's speech is a game attempt at morale-boosting by an exhausted young woman.

Question: How do the minor characters function dramatically in terms of the principals?

Answer: Marina, Maria Vasilievna, and Waffles are all rigid, ignorant people, committed to an unyielding way of life. Marina wants nothing more from life than her meals on time and God in His heaven. Waffles, whose wife ran away the day after the wedding, rigidly hangs on to his false pride in his abiding faithfulness to an adulterous wife. Old Maria Vasilievna has devoted her energies to her son-in-law's pedantry, and even though he now contradicts himself, she will find no fault with him.

These three exemplify the boredom and stupidity in which Vanya and Astroff have been suffocating. They serve as a dramatic balance to the enlightened characters.

If we take the egocentric Serebriakoff as the center, beneath him are the three foolish characters who can neither recognize nor accept change. Above him are Vanya, Astroff, Sonia, and Elena - people of reason and sensibility who recognize what has happened to their lives, and in recognizing it are defeated.

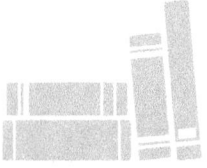

THE THREE SISTERS

INTRODUCTION

On September 9, 1900, Chekhov wrote to his sister: "*The Three Sisters* is very difficult to write, more difficult than my other plays." But unlike his earlier plays, Three Sisters was a moving success in Moscow, where it was staged at the Art Theater in January, 1901. Gorky, Chekhov's brilliant contemporary, singled the play out as the most profound and effective of the author's works. Chekhov had written the part of Masha in *Three Sisters* with his beloved actress, Olga Knipper, in mind. Four months after the play opened he married her.

By the time Chekhov was writing *Three Sisters* his health was so delicate that he was, like the characters in his play, virtually exiled from Moscow. The pace and climate of the city were disastrous for consumption, and his infrequent visits to Moscow for rehearsals and consultations took a great toll on his health. Much of the sisters' yearning for Moscow probably stems from Chekhov's own sorrow at being absent from his adored city.

There is nothing extraordinary about the characters in *Three Sisters*. They are neither musicians, painters, nor great scholars. As the children of old serf-owning families they have grown up in unparalleled leisure. Tusenbach, the officer-Baron, capsulizes the presumption of them all: "I have never worked in my life. I was born in Petersburg, cold, idle Petersburg, in a family that never knew any sort of work or worry. I remember when I came home from military school the footman pulled off my boots while I fidgeted and my mother looked adoringly at me, and was surprised when the others didn't look at me the same way."

But for these genteel people the time has come. "Something tremendous is hovering over us all, a vast, healing storm is gathering." The play is essentially about their inability to weather the storm. Some critics have seen in this philosophy Chekhov's prediction of the revolution. But at his death, in 1904, he scoffed at talk of a revolution - and he died before the "storm" came in 1905, only four years after he wrote the play.

Although the characters are in no way larger than life, their self-importance and vanity prevent them from touching or even hearing each other. How symbolically perfect and true for all the characters is Andrei's outpouring of his pain to old Ferapont - who cannot hear a word he says!

Three Sisters has been called a gloomy play (Chekhov himself, after a misdirected reading at the Art Theater, called it gloomier than gloom). As the critic Robert Brustein points out: "an atmosphere of doom seems to permeate the household, lifted only during brief festive moments." The action of the play results in the triumph of evil and "despite the thick texture of the play ... neatly woven into the tapestry is an almost invisible thread of action: the destruction of the Prozoroffs by Natasha."

And yet, the total effect of *Three Sisters* in not tragic nor even wholly depressing. The new Natasha generation will also build a civilization: and it will teem with children, live by its own sweat, and ultimately produce its saints, scholars, scientists, and heroes.

CHARACTERS

Olga Prozoroff

The oldest sister, twenty-eight, who teaches at a local girls' high school.

Irina Prozoroff

Youngest of the three sisters, lovely and high-spirited object of the affections of the rivals Baron Tusenbach and Solyony.

Masha Prozoroff

Middle sister; unhappily married to a local teacher, Kulygin; melancholy and melodramatic; dressed always in black.

Fyodor Kulygin

Masha's husband; dull, petty, but well-meaning high school teacher.

Andrei Prozoroff

Brother to the three sisters; would be scholar and musician; in love with and later married to Natasha.

Natalia Ivanova (Natasha)

Crude, ambitious, grasping provincial girl, married to Andrei. Later mother of two children.

Alexander Vershinin

Lieutenant colonel and new battery commander; a romantic, unhappily married man who ultimately becomes Masha's lover.

Nikolai Tusenbach

Baron and lieutenant in the army; a nobleman who feels he has never done anything meaningful in life. Eager suitor for Irina's hand.

Vasili Solyony

Staff captain in the army; self-styled Lermontov; romantic, brooding, and asocial.

Ivan Tchebutykin

An old army doctor; longtime friend of the Prozoroffs; inveterate newspaper reader and chain smoker.

Ferapont

Porter of the District Board, a deaf old man.

Anfisa

An old woman of eighty, former nurse, now housekeeper to the sisters.

Alexei Fedotik and Vladimir Roday

Second lieutenants in the army.

ACT I

In a sunny, colonnaded drawing room in the provinces of Russia three sisters remember their father's death exactly a year ago. The youngest of the three, twenty-year-old Irina, by coincidence celebrates her saint's day on the same date. The sisters, originally from Moscow, moved to the provinces eleven years earlier with their widowed father when he was placed in command of a provincial battalion. The middle sister, Masha, had married a local school teacher, Kulygin, when she was just eighteen. At the time had seemed to her the most intelligent of men, but now she finds him boring, dense, and picayune. Olga, the eldest sister, is an old maid at twenty-eight. She teaches at a girls' school but bitterly dreams of peaceful domesticity. The greatest desire of the three is: "To go to Moscow. Sell the house, wind up everything here and go to Moscow."

On this, Irina's name day, several visitors have come to the Prozoroff house to celebrate: Baron Tusenbach, a lieutenant in the army, and a sweet ineffectual suitor of Irina's (who has never worked a day in his life). The Baron talks much of work and the future and tirades against "the laziness, the indifference, the prejudice against work, the rotten boredom" of their lives;

Solyony, an army staff captain and a vicious, brooding antagonist of the Baron's; and the ever-present Tchebutykin, an old army doctor and lifelong friend of the Prozoroff family. The doctor spends his time reading the papers and being nostalgic about the past.

The three sisters have a brother, Andrei, who is the scholarly hope of the family. He aspires to a professorship, plays the violin, and has, much to the sisters' horror, fallen in love with a local girl, Natasha. According to Masha, Natasha is "not merely ugly and out of style, but simply pitiful. Some sort of strange, loud, yellowish skirt with a vulgar fringe and a red blouse. And her cheeks are so scrubbed, scrubbed!"

The sisters talk with their visitors of the necessity of toil and the "vast, healing storm" which is gathering and will ultimately clear their society of its tedium. Their discussion is interrupted by Tchebutykin, who commits a ludicrous faux pas - he presents Irina with a saint's day gift of a silver samovar, a traditional anniversary gift. Absorbed in his sentimental and self-pitying presentation, Tchebutykin is completely unaware of the outrage and embarrassment his ironic breach of protocol has caused.

The entrance of Colonel Vershinin, the new battery commander, relieves the awkward tension. He has come to pay his respects to the sisters, whom he knew as children in Moscow. The romantic colonel, saddled with a suicidal wife and a house full of females, completely charms the sisters. They chatter of the old days in Moscow, and he cheers them with his bright optimism. Someday, says Vershinin, their descendants, the children of the cultured and sensitive, will triumph over the "dark masses" and after hundreds of years "life on earth will be unimaginably beautiful."

Next to enchanting Vershinin, Kulygin, the smug high school teacher, seems pathetic indeed. He comes to the house with a book for Irina: "a history of our high school covering fifty years, written by me." He had given her the same book at Easter.

As they go to the table, Natasha rushes in, late as usual. She is ill at ease and disoriented. Olga bitingly greets her in undertone: "You have on a green belt! My dear, that's not right!" At lunch, Natasha is made so uncomfortable she dashes from the table. Andrei follows her. And in a hidden corner of the drawing room he declares his love, proposes marriage, and as they kiss the curtain falls.

Comment:

As always in Chekhov, the routine and trivial external activity has little to do with what is really happening in the play. In terms of action, there is not much to say: a family dinner with celebrating guests; cultured and charming women bored with the present, dreaming of the past, frightened of the future; the same old conversation: we must work, Andrei's girl friend is dreadful, we must return to Moscow, how could Tchebutykin bring that samovar, Kulygin is so deadly dull; a charming new guest appears; the usual family tensions prevail at luncheon; and then a young man proposes to his "dear, darling, pure one."

The inner life of the act is quite another matter. We are shown an oppressive and dangerous tedium, bearing down on three women whom life has stifled "as weeds do grass." The signs of decay are everywhere. Andrei has grown fat in the year since his father's death, as if his body were "freed from the load" of learning and ambition. Olga suffers from headaches and continual exhaustion. Masha wears black to express her melancholy and murmuringly quotes mournful, mysterious poetry. Only Irina, in her white party dress, is filled with the hope and ambitious vision which once fired them all.

Quiet but seething conflict and ennui underlie the routine trivia. The sisters are fearful and resentful of the stranger Andrei is bringing into their world. Natasha is a product of the "dark masses" which are threatening to obscure the Prozoroffs and all they have lived for. Masha loathes her husband and his petty schoolteacher functions. Her melancholy and disdain break through her reveries in near hysteria. The entire leisured way of life, so protective and encompassing when General Prozoroff was alive, is now beginning to give way. The need for work and purpose, not merely fluency in languages, is making itself felt. But the Prozoroffs are not equipped to face the new reality. Their entire mode of life is being threatened and they have not the means to defend themselves. The dream of returning to Moscow, which has sustained them for a decade, now seems stale and unreachable. They still talk of the dream, but only Irina really believes in it. Olga is bitterly unmarried. Masha is miserably married. Vershinin, with his household of daughters, mother-in-law, and wife is married by law only. Tusenbach hopelessly loves Irina and the old doctor, Tchebutykin, wallows in the love, general and consoling, he bears them all.

Everything essential is awry in the Prozoroff world. The old values and abilities no longer suffice. The new order of work for which they are ill-equipped is tedious and unsatisfying. Love is warped. Gaiety and charm are gone (except for the attempted gallantry of Vershinin), and in their place has come a corrosive frustration and ensnaring tedium.

ACT II

The second act opens a year or two later in the same drawing room. It is eight o'clock in the evening of Carnival Week. Andrei and Natasha are married and have a baby boy. Olga now works at the Teacher's Council and Irina has taken a dismal job, "work without poetry, without thought," at the telegraph office. Andrei, henpecked and indecisive, has given up his dream of teaching at a university, Instead, he is secretary at the local District Board and the very most he can hope for 'is to be a member of the District Board!" In a bitter, shamefaced outburst he confesses to deaf old Ferapont, the porter of the District Board: "I must talk to somebody, but my wife doesn't understand me, and I am afraid of my sisters somehow, I'm afraid they will laugh at me, make me ashamed."

In response to this aching complaint, the unhearing Ferapont tells Andrei a tale of a merchant in Moscow who ate forty or fifty blinies and died. Since Andrei is restricted by Natasha to a glass of buttermilk for dinner ("The doctor says, you're to have nothing but buttermilk or you'll never get any thinner"), the anecdote is more ironically painful than amusing.

Andrei finds respite from his tyrannical wife and depressing life in gambling. He and old Tchebutykin sneak out almost nightly. And each time he goes Andrei doses larger and larger amounts. "The whole town is talking" about the extent of his losses.

Colonel Vershinin too has found an escape from his wife (who has once more decided to scare him by attempting to poison herself). He has fallen madly in love with Masha. Although Masha hesitantly returns his ardor, she is frightened of the implications.

Baron Tusenbach, pessimistic about any change in man's future ("life will remain quite the same, a difficult life, mysterious"), has finally decided to resign his army commission and seek work-honest work. He is persistent and gentle in his courtship to Irina: "Every day I'll come to the telegraph office and see you home, I'll do that for ten, twenty years, for as long as you don't drive me away."

But the Baron now has an unsuspected rival. Solyony, in a passionate outburst, to which Irina responds coldly and with repugnance, cries "I can't live without you . . . I swear to you by all that's holy, I'll kill any rival." Yet neither Tusenbach nor Solyony, for all their ardent pleading, can rouse Irina from her great boredom and weariness.

Of all the members of the household, only Natasha has gained equilibrium - indeed she nears ascendency. She has begun to assume responsibility for the running of the house since Olga and Irina are "always working, poor girls!" She has a baby, Bobik on whom she dotes, and she feels completely at ease in a society from which she was once excluded and into which she will never be fully accepted. Indeed, she is so at ease that she now spouts poorly pronounced French and presumes to criticize her guests. To Masha she hisses: "With your beautiful looks you'd be, I'll tell you candidly, simply charming in a decent, well-bred society, if it weren't for these words of yours." And at Solyony she hurls: "Rude, ill-bred man."

Natasha is still the crude provincial she was, but as Andrei's wife she now has position. The authority of this position she exercises relentlessly. She announces to the expectant celebrants that the maskers (who traditionally come to the house for a party after Carnival) are not to be let in because "Bobik is not at all well." And later she quietly corners Irina to say: "In the nursery Bobik has now, seems to me it's cold and damp. And your room is so good for a child. My dear, my own, move in with Olya for a while! . . . You and Olya will be in one room, for this little while, and your room will be for Bobik."

After everyone has left for the night, disappointed at the cancelled celebration, Natasha dons her fur coat and cap and merrily out for "just a little ride" with Protopopov, the District Board Director, who awaits in his troika.

Irina, left alone and dejected in the dark room cries desperately: "To Moscow! To Moscow! To Moscow!"

Comment:

Essentially, the second act is a "catching-up act. We learn, through isolated dialogues, what has happened to the characters in the intervening year or two. The secondary figures have hardly changed at all. Tusenbach still talks of work and life, although he has at last decided to back words up with action by resigning his commission. Solyony is yet cynical and intense. Tchebutykin reads his papers and demonstrates little interest in the world about him. Kulygin is tiresomely absorbed in his petty school matters.

For the Prozoroffs there has been great but subtle and gradual change. Andrei has given up all hope of a scholar's life. He is despotically ruled by a selfish and greedy wife, whose lover presides at the District Board where he is secretary. Irina, now tediously employed, has grown as weary and dispirited as Olga. And Masha, frightened but eager, is about to fall in love. There are many love declarations in the course of this Carnival evening, but they are all misbegotten. Tusenbach and Solyony -

one patiently, one passionately - pursue the uninterested Irina. Vershinin declares and Masha hints at the love between them, but both are married. Natasha gaily runs off for her illicit ride with Protopopov. But Andrei, married a short while, with a new baby, can only shrug: "One shouldn't marry. One shouldn't, it's boring."

The great tension of this act comes from the inexorable dispossession of the Prozoroffs. They are gradually being alienated from their own home by a foreign force. Their tradition of entertaining the maskers is abruptly ended by the selfish, egocentric Natasha.

Aware of her advantage as the one "productive" Prozoroff, Natasha uses Bobik as a weapon against the sisters. At every turn she praises his infant intelligence and she takes great pleasure in orienting the house around his convenience (and her own). Her usurpation of Irina's room ("She's not at home during the day anyhow, she only spends the night") is so grotesque and ill-mannered that its suggestion leaves Irina even more tired and listless, and fully submissive.

The Prozoroffs have neither the spirit nor the ability to cope with this alien intrusion. They have grown up midst such gentility and refinement, surrounded so totally by people who play by the same rules of the game, that they can only bow, with feeble resistance, to the cunning of the ambitious arriviste.

Natasha, for her part, is reckless and drunk with her new power. She shamelessly and openly trots off with Protopopov (in such great contrast to Masha's caution with Vershinin). She no longer need hear the sisters' condemnation of her crudity and indeed repays their earlier taunts with blind cruelty and roughness. Natasha has nothing to fear. She is married into a good family, she is the leisured head of the household, she has produced an heir, and she is superficially acquiring culture. With the listless, defeated Andrei begrudgingly backing her up, she is driving out the enemy through the use of new and foreign weapons.

ACT III

Two or three years have passed. Irina is "going on twenty-four" and Natasha has a new baby girl. It is three o'clock in the morning and a fire has been raging all night in the town. The action of the act takes place in Olga and Irina's cluttered, crowded bedroom upstairs. The noises of the fire are audible in the background. All through the act people rush in and out of the room in the confusion and bedlam caused by the disaster.

Olga, during the crisis, has once again, temporarily, assumed control. She arranges for clothing and shelter to be given to the homeless. But there is hysteria and fatigue in her words: "Nursey, dear, give everything away. We don't need anything. Give everything away! Nursey . . . I'm tired."

Natasha, on the other hand, is cool and detached during the frenzied night, She talks of someday forming a relief society for those who have been burnt out. But her main concern in that the people milling about will bring influenza and other diseases that the children will catch. As Natasha primps before a mirror ("They say I have filled out . . And it isn't true!"), she and Olga have a bitter argument about the old nurse, Anfisa. Natasha says Anfisa is useless in the house ("She is a peasant, she should live in the country"), and in an uncontrollable outburst she screams ("By tomorrow there won't be this old thief here, this old hag . . . Don't dare cross me! Don't you dare!") Olga, bewildered and sickened by Natasha's rudeness and crudity, protests that Anfisa has been with them for thirty years.

Tchebutykin, in this tormented night, gets drunk for the first time in two years. He confesses that a woman under his care has died two days ago and he no longer knows or understands anything about medicine or life. In his confusion he drops and shatters an old family clock and then, hiding behind his drunkenness, pronounces aloud that Natasha is having an affair with Protopopov.

In the midst of the turmoil, Vershinin takes time to philosophize about the paradise to come in two or three hundred years. In his "singular mood" he begins to hum a tune which Masha, humming, completes.

The Baron, now a civilian, announces that he'll soon be going to the brickyard and begs Irina: "Oh, come along with me, let's go to work together!" In the meantime, Kulygin naively protests his love for Masha, muttering over and over: "I am content, I am content, I am content."

Andrei, who sits in his room and pays not the least attention to the fire, has grown small and "dried up and aged beside that woman." He is now a proud member of the Board of which Protopopov is chairman. His debts have grown so large that he has mortgaged the house without consulting the sisters, and Natasha has grabbed all the money.

Of them all, the greatest change is in Irina. She is miserable. She has forgotten everything she knew ("I don't remember what in Italian window is") she knows that she will never go to Moscow, and she is drying up with "nothing - no satisfaction of any kind." Olga pathetically advises her to marry the Baron:

"It's true he's not good looking, but he's so decent and clean . . . Why, one doesn't marry for love but to do one's duty." As the conversation turns to love, Masha confesses to her sisters her great passion for Vershinin: "When you fall in love yourself, you begin to see that nobody knows anything and everybody must decide for himself." A few moments later she answers Vershinin's song from beyond the room and quietly goes to him.

As everyone leaves the room - Andrei sobbing with desperation and frustration, Masha to meet her lover, Kulygin looking for Masha, Solyony to sulk at his rejection by Irina, Tusenbach with dreams that he might someday give his life for Irina, Tchebutykin to nurse his coming hangover, Natasha to close up the house - when they have all left and the fire has subsided, Irina calls from her bed to Olga: "Darling, precious, I respect, I value the Baron, he's a marvelous person, I'll marry him. I consent, only let's go to Moscow! I beg you, let's go! There's nothing in the world better than Moscow! Let's go, Olya! Let's go!

Comment:

If a Chekhov play can have a **climax**, then the night of the fire is the **climax** of *The Three Sisters*. Every dream of the Prozoroffs is burnt out while the town is being devastated by flames. After this night both the town and the Prozoroffs will lie in ruins.

In her confrontation with Natasha, Olga is made to face, though it sickens her, the cruel realities which now govern her once genteel home. Natasha screams that old Anfisa "is not up to doing any sort of work, she just sleeps and sits." And Olga, from the depths of her gentle past can only say: "But let her sit." Natasha does not understand such impractical loyalty. She is tearful at her own inability to summon such sensibility and at the same time she is furious at Olga for being blinded to the modern practicalities. Olga, for her part, is depressed and ill. "Perhaps we were brought up strangely, but I can't bear it . . . Every rudeness, even the slightest, even a word indelicately spoken, upsets me." Clearly Olga has not the strength nor the means to fight this new kind of warfare.

Old Tchebutykin, drunk and guilty, knows he is no longer a good doctor but he now questions whether he is even a man or if, indeed he exists at all. For him life is over: "Oh, that I didn't exist!" And his dreams, like the clock he shatters, lie in smashed ruins.

Andrei has surrendered, not only his own dreams, but his sisters' as well when he mortgaged the house and gave the money to Natasha.

For the sisters, the visions of productive, romantic love and a useful life in Moscow are totally abandoned. Masha, frantic for relief from the boring Kulygin, has fantasized a perfect lover out of the garrulous and not altogether genuine Vershinin. On the night of the fire she abandons all hope of a pure and mutual love, since nothing can come of her romance with the colonel. Poor Olga, who four years ago had said with vehemence. "If I had married and stayed at home . . . I'd have loved my husband," now compromises: "At any rate I'd marry anyone who proposed to me so long as he was an honorable man. I'd marry even an old man." And Irina, who dreamed of moving to Moscow and meeting her "real beloved," now consents to marry the eager, earnest, totally joyless Baron.

Robbed of their dreams, their hopes, and even their property, the Prozoroffs, like their town, are reduced to ashes.

ACT IV

It is the time of year when it might "snow any minute" and the birds of passage are flying already. Winter is coming. The Prozoroffs and their few friends staying behind bid farewell to the army officers. The brigade has been transferred to Poland and is to leave in an hour.

The farewells in the garden of the Prozoroff house are painful. The officers fear they will never see their friends again, and the civilians fear they will perish of boredom without their officers. Irina and the Baron are to be married the next day and then they will leave for the brickyard where the Baron will start a new life and Irina will teach school. Olga has become headmistress of the local school and lives at the school in an apartment with Anfisa. Protopopov has taken to calling at the house each day, and during his "calls" Andrei paces in the garden pushing a baby carriage.

Solyony and the Baron have had an argument, and Solyony has challenged Tusenbach to a duel -to be fought within the hour. As he goes to meet Solyony, the Baron bids his unsuspecting fiancee a dramatic farewell to which she cannot respond. "I'll be your wife, faithful and obedient, but it's not love, what is there to do!"

Masha's farewell to Vershinin is violent and moving. As she sobs uncontrollably, pathetic Kulygin moves in to comfort her ("I don't make you a single reproach").

Natasha has plans for the future. When everyone has gone she will cut down the alley of fir trees and a huge old maple tree, "and I'll order flowers planted, everywhere, flowers."

As the sad music of the departing regiment is heard in the distance, Tchebutykin arrives with the news that the Baron has been killed in the duel. The sisters huddle together. In litany like fashion they murmur: "The time will come when all will know why all this is." "A little more and we shall know why we live, why we suffer." "If we only knew, if we only knew."

Comment:

The dispossession of the Prozoroffs is now complete. Olga lives in a government apartment in the town, Masha will no longer set foot in Natasha's roost, and Irina, from the boredom and loneliness of living alone, is getting married and moving to the brickyard. Andrei, who oddly still loves his wife, confesses that "there's something in her that reduces her to the level of some sort of petty, blind, coarse animal. In any case, she's not a human being." He is exiled to the garden with one or another baby carriage to push, while Natasha "entertains" Protopopov.

With the departure of the regiment and the death of the Baron, the old life ends for the sisters. They will live, they must live, and maybe the future will sort out their sufferings and make some meaning or use of it. For themselves, they can only wonder about its significance.

The last act has the dramatic sense of doomed fatality. Even the alley of fir trees, which for generations has formed a path to the river, is soon to fall beneath the axe of the new generation. Natasha finds the old firs and maples "so ugly" in the evening. The "birds of passage are flying already" away from the house to warmer climates. Only the birds who have "grown old, that can't fly" are left behind. By the end of the play the Prozoroffs are such birds - none has the means to fly. Irina has lost her chance for escape with the Baron's death; Masha has lost her great love and happiness; and Olga is trapped as headmistress at a government school. Andrei will be left alone with a hateful present in the deserted house. For company he has a bestial wife and her lover and the comfort of a light dawning in the future where he and his children will be free from idleness.

For all its pathos and frustration, the finale of the play is not wholly depressing. As the sisters chant their litany - ("They are leaving us . . . entirely, forever. We'll be left alone to begin our life over again. We must live." "Our sufferings will turn into joy for those who will be living after us . . . we shall live!") - as they gather strength to face the future we sense that they will, after all, survive. Irina will go to the brickyards to teach, Olga will retain her position as headmistress, and Masha will make the most of her dull marriage. They are greatly changed by the "evil" which has invaded their lives and ultimately turned them out - but they are alive and young enough to adjust to the changing world if they have the will.

Natasha clearly will thrive. Her adored children will flourish "freed from idleness, from kvass, from goose with cabbage, from naps after dinner, from despicable sloth." They will be equipped to take their place in the world after the "vast, healing storm" has passed.

As sympathetic as we are to the Prozoroffs, they are not, for their part, totally admirable. They have survived in a narrow and selfish world, by closing their eyes to the universe around them. They are so concerned with their own fortunes and futures that news of "Two thousand people . . . . frozen" in Petersburg makes absolutely no impression on them, and in fact is not even heard.

The Prozoroffs and their gallant officers are a selfish and not very remarkable lot. They rarely listen to each other's words and when they dream, their dreams are for themselves alone, for their own self-satisfaction and fulfillment.

Chekhov, with his great humanity, has looked tenderly and sympathetically at the Prozoroffs. We are deeply moved by their unhappy lot. But we do not, in the end, despair for the future of mankind. The fall of the Prozoroffs is not crucial enough for that.

ANALYSIS OF SELECTED CHARACTERS

Olga

As the oldest of the sisters, Olga is the head of the household (until she is driven out by Natasha). She is thin, tired, and afflicted with headaches. Her bitter weariness during the four years is unchanging, and by the end she is utterly defeated, with nothing to look forward to but years of boredom as the spinster headmistress of a local school. Only on rare occasions, such a Vershinin's Act I entrance, does Olga brighten and even then it is short-lived as she remembers the burden of the future and her dismal role in it.

Masha

The middle sister, who seems older than her twenty-one years when we first see her, is the melancholy and dramatic Prozoroff. She quotes mysterious poetry in whispers and always wears black -much like the Masha in *The Seagull*, who is in mourning for her life. The brief and passionate romance with Vershinin is Masha's one great effort to break away from her stifling life with Kulygin. When it ends, she returns home with Kulygin in utter defeat. Masha's love for Vershinin is more a matter of desperate self-deception than genuine affection. The colonel is, after all, a pompous, garrulous, selfish man who returns Masha's passion when it is convenient, and when he must go is eager to get away without fuss. Masha's need for romance created an ideal lover of Vershinin, and the affair was a receptacle for her unfulfilled passion and sense of the dramatic.

Irina

Irina is the baby of the family. At the outset she is gay, optimistic, and fervent about life. The others treat her, even to the end, more as a child than a woman. Of the three, Irina suffers most and changes most. From the gay little celebrant on her saint's day she becomes a weary, dispirited telegraph operator. When she decides, with much misgiving and compromise, to marry the foolish Baron, though she can never love him, she is making the ultimate concession of her life. When even this great compromise is foiled, she is left with nothing. Irina vows she will go alone to the brickyard to teach - but the life we imagine she will lead there - solitary and dreary - is infinitely removed from her original bright dreams.

Andrei

As the only male Prozoroff, Andrei is the repository of all hope and ambition. The abandonment of his career as a Moscow professor, in favor of a cuckolded District Board member, heralds the total defeat of the Prozoroffs. Andrei submits, with amazing docility, to Natasha's tyranny. Always meek and scholarly, as her husband he becomes a baby sitter, a messenger, a totally dominated and malleable convenience.

Natasha

Marriage into the Prozoroff family represents total victory for Natasha. She is a social climbing, crude, spiteful, untutored small-town girl. She is, in short, the embodiment of every evil from which the Prozoroffs had been shielded all their lives. She uses anyone she can find for her own convenience and ambition - even poor old Anfisa, who can no longer offer vigorous service. Natasha's pretensions and presumptions are fantastic when she gains ascendancy. Her position becomes so powerful that she grows impervious to the hate and scorn she inspires, and although at times she is bewildered by the delicacy of the sisters' feelings (a delicacy she can never possess) she overcomes the bewilderment through exercise of power and shrewdness.

Tchebutykin

The old army doctor is a drinker, a smoker, and a refreshing cynic. His sloth and indifference lend perspective to the intensity of feeling surrounding him. He finally hides behind the nihilism of his own nonexistence and so hardens himself against the blows which life might deal him.

Tusenbach

The earnest, well-meaning Baron is honest in his intensions to sweat for his bread, and he is one of the few characters to back words with action. His death by duel is clearly the most romantic and dramatic event of his leisured life.

Vershinin

At the outset, Vershinin, with his bright talk of the future and memories of Moscow, is a cleansing wind for the becalmed household. But his egocentric chatter and platitudes, his boredom and complaints, expose him for a romantic poseur, more seeming than substance,

Solyony

The young staff captain, moody, taunting, and strange, pictures himself as a misunderstood Lermontov. His duel with the Baron is senseless and anachronistic, but no doubt satisfies his yearning to startle and dramatize.

ESSAY QUESTIONS AND ANSWERS

Question: In what way does love play a major role in the action of the play?

Answer: There are numerous varieties of love in *The Three Sisters*: filial love that is echoed in the memories of General Prozoroff; brotherly and sisterly love; the romantic love of Tusenbach for Irina, of Andrei for Natasha; the grasping "love" of Natasha; the illicit love of Natasha for Protopopov and of Masha for Vershinin. Solyony is a rejected lover; Kulygin dotes on his wife who ignores him. Even Tchebutykin loved the sister's mother, and never tires of mentioning it.

Most of the complications of the plot involve love relationships. Andrei loves Natasha much to the sisters' chagrin, for they love him and would not have him marry beneath him.

We see a good deal of selfishness interwoven with love; in this case the sisters have no consideration for Andrei's happiness.

Tusenbach loves Irina and will marry her though she doesn't return his love. And both had begun with the highest dreams of romance! Solyony, ultrasensitive, takes Irina's rejection as a slight on his own character, and this leads to the duel in which the Baron dies. Irina had been willing to settle for less than a fulfillment of her romantic dreams, but Solyony, through love, prevents even this chance for a new beginning.

Masha's love for Vershinin and her betrayal of her dull but loyal husband is doomed to end in unhappiness. Vershinin is more interested in playing the part of the lover, in escaping from a hysterical wife and female household, and in the least excuse to talk endlessly, than he is in love. Like Irina's, Masha's hopes are destroyed by Vershinin's inevitable departure.

There is a second illicit love affair, that of Natasha and Protopopov, which takes place offstage. Natasha married Andrei for social advancement. The only kind of love she is capable of is motherly solicitation. Chekhov's typically painful comedy is nowhere clearer than in the situation of Andrei, a musician and scholar, becoming the dupe of this powerful and grasping woman.

At the end of the play the three sisters cling to each other. Irina's fiancee is dead; Masha's lover is gone; no one has ever even proposed to poor Olga. Love, misbegotten love, and the lack of love are major motivations for the action of *The Three Sisters*.

Question: How does Chekhov handle the sense of time in *The Three Sisters*?

Answer: For the Prozoroff household there is no time present. The present is so unbearable to the sisters and Andrei that they live in perpetual reminiscing of the past (of the good old days in Moscow, of how different and sure life was when their father was alive) or in idle dreams of the future.

The past merges with the future, squeezing out the realities of the present. The Prozoroffs are not capable of dealing with their daily lives, with the necessities the changing world imposes on them. They must fantasize what life will be like when all this is over, although they cannot, or will not, participate in the making of the beautiful future.

So vague is the Prozoroff sense of the present that the passage of time in the play is blurred and uncertain. From the Prozoroffs themselves we could never determine how long it was from Irina's saint's day to the Baron's death. Only the birth of Natasha's children clearly marks that interval - a period of some four years.

Even with all their dreams destroyed, the sisters still talk of the future, of the time when all their suffering will be understood and meaningful. Their very inability to see the present clearly or accept its realities destroyed all possibilities of a fulfilled present for the Prozoroff family.

THE CHERRY ORCHARD

INTRODUCTION

For the season of 1902-1903, the Moscow Art Theater had a new building with revolving stage, advanced lighting effects, and spacious quarters for the actors. The Theater's directors very much hoped that Chekhov would give them a new play to inaugurate the season. But in January of 1902, Chekhov wrote to his wife: "I have no faith yet in the play. It has hardly dawned in my brain, like the first glow of sunrise, and I don't know myself what it is to be, what will come of it."

By the winter of 1902, Chekhov was extremely ill. Days on end he battled with his broken health and frequently he was too weak to take up the pen. *The Cherry Orchard* took Chekhov three painful years from conception to performance, and all the time he wrote he knew it would probably be his last major effort. When the play was finished, it was scheduled to open on January 17, 1904, Chekhov's birthday. This was also the date which marked Chekhov's twenty-fifth year as a writer.

To celebrate the date, Chekhov's friends planned a huge jubilee to take place between the third and fourth acts of the premiere performance. An impressive program of speeches and presentations was arranged, with many prominent people taking part in the tribute. Sometime during the course of the early acts, someone made an incredible discovery. Chekhov was not in the theater! It was not only his illness which kept him away, but his shyness and embarrassment at being singled out in public. When he was finally fetched to the theater, he stood on the platform, pale, weak, and consumptive, and received "an ovation, so lavish, warm and really so unexpected" that he would never get over it.

The Cherry Orchard was at first only a mediocre success. Stanislavsky, the Moscow Art Theater's director, had insisted on playing the piece as a social tragedy - as a depressing drama of the passing of the old order. The critics had followed Stanislavsky's lead in this interpretation and found the play tedious.

Chekhov was furious at the misinterpretation. He insisted over and over again: "I have written not a drama, but a comedy, in parts a farce." In discussing the gloominess of Stanislavsky's reading, Chekhov said: "Is this really my Cherry Orchard? Are these my types? With the exception of two or three roles, none of this is mine. I describe life. It is a dull, philistine life. But it is not a tedious, whimpering life. First they turn me into a weeper and then into a simply boring writer.... Criticism has tricked me out in the guise of some kind of mourner or other."

Apparently in later performances the Art Theater modified its interpretation, and when the play opened in Petersburg on April 2, 1904, it was a great success. *The Cherry Orchard* has stayed in the Art Theater's repertoire and remains one of its most popular productions.

Today it is the most widely known, internationally, of Chekhov's plays, and as his last play, it stands as his final dramatic statement.

CHARACTERS

Lyuboff Ranevskaya

An elderly woman. A landowner. Her husband has died and her lover in Paris has deserted her. A good-natured, flighty woman.

Anya

Lyuboff's seventeen-year-old daughter. An innocent, idealistic girl in love with Trofimoff.

Varya

Lyuboff's adopted daughter. At twenty-four, she manages the estate, dreams of going to a nunnery, but also loves Lopahin.

Leonid Gayeff

Lyuboff's brother. A middle-aged man who talks too much and works not at all.

Yermolay Lopahin

A rich merchant whose father and grandfather were serfs on Gayeff's estate.

Pyotr Trofimoff

A perpetual student of twenty-eight, who had been tutor to Mme. Ranevskaya's drowned son.

Boris Semyonoff-Pishtchik

A neighboring landowner forever in debt, out of debt, and in again.

Charlotta Ivanovna

An eccentric governess who performs tricks.

Semyon Epihodoff

Clerk on Gayeff's estate. A stumbler and bumbler in love with Dunyasha.

Fiers

A valet, an old man of eighty-seven.

Yasha

A young valet who has traveled with Mme. Ranevskaya and taken on airs.

Dunyasha

A maid who imitates her employers.

ACT I

Setting: A room that is still called the nursery. Dawn, the sun will soon be rising. It is May, the cherry trees are in blossom but in the orchard it is cold, with a morning frost. The windows in the room are closed.

Madame Lyuboff Ranevskaya has been away from her family estate in the provinces of Russia for more than five years. She had left it six years ago when in one month her husband died and her seven-year-old son, Grisha, drowned in the river. Lyuboff had been so distraught at the double tragedy that "she went away, went away without ever looking back."

She has been living in France all this time, but her brother Gayeff has summoned her home. The family has run out of money and in order to pay the mortgage the estate is to be auctioned in a few months' time. Ranevskaya's younger daughter Anya, who lives with her uncle Gayeff, had been sent with a governess to Paris to bring her mother home. When the play opens the train bringing them back has just arrived at the station two hours late.

At the house, the great homecoming is eagerly awaited by Lopahin, a rich merchant, Fiers, an ancient and deaf family valet, Dunyasha, a maid who has taken on the pretensions of a lady, and Epihodoff, the verbose clerk of the estate. The other members of the household have gone to meet the train.

The group finally arrives from the station and there is much commotion. Ranevskaya eagerly and sentimentally pokes around the house in which she grew up and raised her family. Anya, exhausted from her four-day train trip, is desperate for sleep and yet rejoices to be home again and see her sister Varya and her Uncle Gayeff. The others busy themselves with carrying luggage and exchanging news.

Anya and Varya have a tender reunion in which Anya tells of her dreadful trip to Paris: "We arrived in Paris; it was cold there and snowing. I speak terrible French. Mama lived on the fifth floor; I went to see her; there were some French people in her room, ladies, an old priest with his prayer book, and the place was full of tobacco smoke - very dreary. Suddenly I began to feel sorry for Mama.... Her villa near Mentone she had finally sold, she had nothing left, nothing. And I didn't have a kopeck left. It was all we could do to get here." But despite the poverty, Mme. Ranevskaya has been spending her money as though she is still a very rich woman.

Varya, who is extremely religious and at twenty-four has been left to manage a bankrupt estate, has fallen in love with the merchant Lopahin - but he has no time for her. Lopahin is the son and grandson of serfs who had worked for Ranevskaya's family. Being extremely ambitious and having acquired refinement, Lopahin has been a great success as a merchant. He is very rich, very gentlemanly, although he has not quite reached the point of understanding the books he reads nor appreciating the beauties of nature.

Lopahin is leaving the next day for business in Kharkov. But before he leaves he tells Mme. Ranevskaya his plan for saving the estate: "Your estate is only thirteen miles from town. They've run the railroad by it. Now if the cherry orchard and the land along the river were cut up into building lots and leased for summer cottages, you'd have at the very least twenty-five thousand roubles per year income.... The location is wonderful, the river's so deep. Except, of course, it all needs to be tidied up, cleared - for instance, let's say, tear all the old buildings down and this house, which is no good any more, and cut down the old cherry orchard-"

The reaction is shock and incredulity: "If there's one thing in the whole province that's interesting -not to say remarkable - it's our cherry orchard"; "the orchard is even mentioned in the encyclopedia"; "what rot!" Lopahin urges that this is the only way to save themselves from bankruptcy, but the family scoffs and changes the subject.

As various members of the household retire for the night, Gayeff and Lyuboff reminisce about their childhood and dwell on the beauties of the orchard in bloom. Suddenly, Trofimoff, Grisha's old tutor, appears. He is still a student but he has begun to age. His "hair's not very thick any more" and he wears glasses. The sight of her dead son's tutor brings back the whole flood of emotion which had driven Lyuboff away, but she is gracious to Trofimoff.

Later, when Gayeff discusses the family's plight with his nieces, he reassures them with three alternative plans. He will make a loan from a friend on a promissory note; Lopahin will lend them money; Anya will go to Yaroslavl to try to borrow money from a rich old aunt living there. All three plans are absurd, but the girls convince themselves that things will work out.

As Varya tells Anya of the difficulties she has had running the estate without money, Anya falls asleep. Varya leads her into the bedroom and Trofimoff, left alone, exclaims tenderly: "My little sun! My Spring!"

Comment

That anyone could have interpreted *The Cherry Orchard* as a somber tragedy is remarkable in light of the numerous comic characterizations we are given in the first act alone. At the very outset we see Dunyasha, a maid, attempting to imitate a delicate lady. Her hands shake, she pretends she is going to faint, she does herself up like a lady of leisure. And Dunyasha's suitor, the ludicrously verbose Epihodoff, is a comic character of farcical dimensions.

Called twenty-two misfortunes, Epihodoff stumble over something every time he turns around, drops whatever he happens to be carrying, and talks nonsense at a nonstop rate.

Charlotta, the would-be governess, is a walking sight gag. She sports on a chain a little dog who eats nuts, she ceaselessly performs tricks, and she dresses in absurd clothes with a lorgnette dangling from her belt.

Yasha, the butler, is Charlotta's male counterpart. Having traveled in Europe with Mme. Ranevskaya, he now affects incredible airs. He flits about in an airy manner and thinks himself quite the handsome gentleman. When he is told that his mother has been sitting in the servant's hall for two days waiting for his return he mutters: "The devil take her! . . . A lot I need her!" Yasha is a caricature of pretention and phoniness.

As if these four were not enough, there is the ludicrous neighbor, Boris Borisovich Semyonoff-Pishtchik -his name alone is a one-line gag. Pishtchik is a good-natured bumbler who fumbles his way through life's vicissitudes. He wavers between utter poverty and incredible good fortune. Right now he is poor, and beseeches the bankrupt Lyuboff for a loan. (She is so foolish, she gives it to him.)

The major characters themselves, whom we are invited to take seriously, are riddled with quirks and absurdities. Gayeff has grown so foolish that at fifty-one one almost thinks him senile. He is forever popping hard candies in his mouth, and from nowhere will suddenly enact an imaginary billiards game. In the middle of a sentence he will interrupt with: "I cut into the side pocket." Gayeff talks too much, to the point of prattling. At one point his sentiment so carries him away that he addresses a long and meaningless speech to an old bookcase.

Gayeff's sister is also foolish. In a state of utter poverty she is yet throwing money about as in the days of plenty. Ranevskaya is sweet and charming, but ludicrously out of touch with the realities of the world about her. She had married a lawyer and not a nobleman, and, as her brother comments: "behaved herself, you could say, not very virtuously."

And yet, despite their foibles and absurdities, these people are not altogether comic. They are gentle, well-meaning people whose entire leisured way of life is about to be destroyed by the practicalities of a new generation that has no time for their foolishness.

The impending sale for the orchard and estate is the central event to which each character relates. And each one's mode of relating to the sale serves as a characterization. Old Fiers, an ancient valet, lives wholly in his past. Deaf and grumbly, he remembers the orchard when it produced wagonloads of processed dried cherries which were shipped for profit to Moscow and Kharkov. Lyuboff and Gayeff equate the orchard in bloom with their childhood happiness and innocence. For them "it was just as it is now, then, nothing has changed." Of course, everything has changed, but they have foolishly failed to recognize it. Lyuboff cannot even think about the descending doom. Gayeff prods himself into dreaming up impractical solutions.

Varya, who has been saddled with the estate's management, would like to be rid of it one way or another so that she would be free to travel from "one holy place to another."

Lopahin, who has generously "forgotten" that his father was a serf on the estate, offers the only solution that is in tune with the times. He has no attachment to the estate and sees it as a fine moneymaking venture.

Thus we have a continuum of relationship. Fiers thinks of the trees in their original capacity of fruit-bearing, income-bringing crops; Lyuboff and Gayeff remember them as beautiful works of natural art to be appreciated by their own leisured sensibilities; Varya finds the orchard a trying, expensive burden; and Lopahin envisions great profit, not as Fiers does from their fruit, but from their destruction.

Of all the symbols Chekhov used, the orchard is the most fully incorporated into the structure of the play and the revelation of its characters. In this first act the orchard serves as a focal point around which the characters arrange themselves, thus revealing themselves. Later in the play the orchard will function as a sociological and philosophical emblem.

ACT II

Setting: A field. An old chapel, long abandoned, with crooked walls; near it a well, big stones that apparently were once tombstones; an old bench. A road to Gayeff's estate can be seen. The sun will soon be down.

Enough time has passed to allow for Anya's trip to Yaroslavl to ask the rich old aunt for help. She has promised to send some money. Yasha, the dandy butler, has seduced Dunyasha but she has not completely discouraged Epihodoff from his suit. Anya has fallen in love with the student Trofimoff.

The act opens with the four comic characters, Charlotta, Dunyasha, Epihodoff, and Yasha sitting on the bench in the field. But as soon as they start talking we recognize the sadness which has touched all of their lives. They are as poignant as they are silly. Charlotta, who is adjusting the strap of the rifle she wears on her shoulder, suddenly launches into her sad tale. "I have no proper passport, I don't know how old I am - it always seems to me I'm very young." When Charlotta was little her father and mother were traveling performers and she joined in their act. When they died, she was brought up by a German woman but she has no idea who her parents were or even if they were married. "I'd like so much to talk but there's not anybody. I haven't anybody."

Even Epihodoff, "twenty-two misfortunes," is touching in his foolishness. That morning he had awakened to find a huge spider on his chest, and when he took a drink of kvass there was a cockroach floating in it. "I am a cultured man," he asserts, "but the trouble is I cannot discover . . . whether to live or shoot myself."

When other members of the household arrive, talk immediately turns to the momentary auction of the orchard. Lopahin urgently insists they say yes or no to the summer-cottage proposal. Lyuboff immediately changes the subject. Lopahin tells them that a rich merchant is coming to the auction in person to buy the estate. Lyuboff and Gayeff mutter about the aunt in Yaroslavl and will hear no more: "Summer cottages and summer residents - it is so trivial, excuse me," dismisses Lyuboff. Wanting Lopahin to stay ("With you here it is more cheerful anyhow"), Lyuboff begins to tell him of her sinful life.

"I've always thrown money around like mad . . . and I married a man who accumulated nothing but debts. My husband died from champagne . . . I fell in love with another man . . . I lived with him, and just at that time . . . right here in the river my boy was drowned . . . I shut my eyes, ran away . . . and he after me. I bought a villa near Mentone, because he fell ill there." For three years Lyuboff exhausted herself tending her sick lover. Finally she had to sell the villa for debts and when they went to Paris the lover robbed her of everything and then threw her over for another woman. Lyuboff had tried to poison herself, "so stupid, so shameful," and suddenly she wanted to return home. Just now Lyuboff has received a telegram from Paris: "He asks forgiveness, begs me to return." She tears up the telegram.

Lopahin is moved to his own confession: "It must be said frankly this life of ours is idiotic - my father was a peasant, and idiot, he understood nothing, he taught me nothing, he just beat me. . . . At bottom I am just as big a dolt and idiot as he was."

Even Fiers is bewildered by his life. In the old days "the peasants stuck to the masters, the masters stuck to the peasants, and now everything is all smashed up, you can't tell about anything."

The young people, Varya, Anya, and Trofimoff, interrupt the melancholy. Trofimoff, with his scholarly air, derides the old way of life, and the inability to work for a better way. "The great majority of the intelligentsia that I know are looking for nothing, doing nothing, and as yet have no capacity for work." They "treat the peasants like animals . . . about science they just talk, about art they understand very little." While the intelligentsia talk, the workmen live in moral and physical squalor "And apparently with us, all the fine talk is only to divert the attention of ourselves and of others."

When Trofimoff and Anya are left alone (which they rarely are because Varya follows them about) they discuss their idealistic goals "to sidestep the petty and illusory." Anya is transported by his fervor: "What have you done to me, Petya, why don't I love the cherry orchard any longer the way I used to?"

He tells her that "from every cherry in the orchard, from every leaf, from every trunk" human beings who had been slaves are looking at her. The past can only be atoned for by suffering and work, and then perhaps the future will be better. The intense talk of a better world is interrupted by Varya calling them, lest they should be alone too long.

Comment

Chekhov's gentle sympathy shines through this act. No one except the pretentious Yasha is held wholly in contempt. It is the poignancy of these people's suffering, loneliness, and isolation which lends the air of tragedy to their comic exteriors. They are too foolish at times to be wholly tragic, but they are also too filled with human misery to be wholly comic.

Each member of the household, from the muttering Fiers to the once munificent Lyuboff, is shown in a sympathetic light. Fiers, whose marriage had been planned before Lyuboff's father was born, still lives in a world governed by the rules of slavery. He cannot adjust, in his old age, to the new rules and relationships. He is a relic that no one wants anymore.

Charlotta, for all her eccentricities, lives in desperate isolation: "Where I came from and who I am I don't know." Dunyasha, who as a girl was taken into the master's house, has "lost the habit of simple living." She is afraid of everything.

Her affectations have made her frail. Lopahin, rich, ambitious, sure of his direction, is not yet sure of himself: "I wasn't taught anything, my handwriting is vile, I write like a pig - I am ashamed for people to see it." Trofimoff, pontificating and superior, has a dream of a righteous world to which he is willing to dedicate his life. And Lyuboff, flighty, scatterbrained, and thoughtless, has sacrificed her life to a selfish, deceptive lover who broke her spirit, emptied her purse, and deserted her.

While these people go through their overt comic businesses (Lyuboff giving gold to strangers at the same moment she borrows for her own food; Gayeff playing his imaginary billiards games; Fiers making absurd answers to questions he cannot hear), while they appear to be ludicrous, there is a strong undercurrent of pathos, of sympathy for frailty which cannot be ignored.

On the surface, little happens to advance the action. Gayeff and Lyuboff still act as though a miracle will descend and save them and their estate. Lopahin still urges immediate action on the cottage rentals. Varya still waits for Lopahin's proposal. But the sense of approaching doom lends a tension and urgency to the act. The very inaction provides the drama.

It has often been said that Trofimoff, in his two long speeches, is Chekhov's spokesman. Although it is highly unlikely that Chekhov would use as his mouthpiece a pompous, verbose, perpetual student who declares himself to be "above love," there is no doubt that in Trofimoff's dreams we hear some of Chekhov's pet criticisms of Russian society. How can man have pride "if in the great majority he is crude, unintelligent, profoundly miserable." "One must work and must help with all one's might those who seek the truth." The intellectuals talk a great deal, "talk of nothing but important things, philosophize, and all the time everybody can see that the workmen eat abominably, sleep without any pillows, thirty or forty to a room, and everywhere there are bedbugs, stench, dampness, moral uncleanliness."

These speeches of Trofimoff and the later one about possessing living souls "that depraved all of you who lived before and are living now" were even stronger in earlier versions of *The Cherry Orchard*. For obvious reasons, amidst the political ferment in Russia in 1904, the censor deleted the most offensive and vitriolic lines. Enough remains, however, to show clearly that while Chekhov sympathized with the frailties of the members of Gayeff's household, and while he does not condemn, he had a different vision from theirs of what a happy world would be like.

ACT III

Setting: The drawing room, separated by an arch from the ballroom. A chandelier is lighted. An orchestra is playing. It is evening. In the ballroom they are dancing grand rond.

Although there is no money to pay the musicians, Lyuboff has planned a ball with a local orchestra. The guests are not the landed neighbors - they no longer come to the house - but the post-office clerk, the stationmaster, and the servants.

It is evening of the day the estate is to be auctioned, and the household waits impatiently for the return of Gayeff and Lopahin who have gone to town for the sale. Everyone is quarrelsome and on edge.

Pishtchik, as always in need of money, has a run-in with Trofimoff, who tells him: "If the energy you have wasted in the course of your life trying to find money ... had gone to something else, you could very likely have turned the world upside down."

To ease the tension, Charlotta performs some of her famous tricks and everyone is momentarily diverted.

But as soon as she leaves the bickering resumes. Trofimoff teases Varya by calling her "Madame Lopahin." Varya retorts: "Perennial student! You have already been expelled from the University twice." The truth is, of course, that Lopahin has been too busy to propose, and Varya can't find enough money to retreat to a nunnery.

In the comings and goings between the ballroom and drawing room, Lyuboff and Trofimoff are alone for a moment. They argue with vehemence, and each ridicules the essence of the other's life. Trofimoff patronizes: "Whether the estate is sold today or is not sold - is it not the same? . . . One mustn't deceive oneself, one must for once at least in one's life look truth straight in the eye." Lyuboff bitterly replies: "You boldly decide all important questions, but tell me, my dear boy, isn't that because you are young and haven't had time yet to suffer through any one of your problems?"

Trofimoff has no sympathy for Lyuboff. He cannot concern himself with her anguish at the sale of the orchard. Nor can he tolerate her illusions about her sick lover who has begged her to return to Paris and look after him. "He is ill, he is alone, unhappy and who will look after him there . . . who will give him his medicine on time? . . . It's a stone about my neck . . . but I love that stone and live without it I cannot" Trofimoff has no patience: "Why, he picked your bones. . . . He is a petty scoundrel, a nonentity." Lyuboff, threatened and pained, yells: "There is no purity in you; you are simply smug, a ridiculous crank, a freak."

The argument was like a moment of truth in charade. As he dashes out, Trofimoff trips and falls down the stairs. The stationmaster recites a poem, the dancing resumes, Fiers prattles on about the old days, Pishtchik once more asks for a loan as he waltzes.

And then suddenly Varya begins to fight with Epihodoff. Screaming, she orders him to leave. He finally does. But thinking he is coming back, Varya picks up a stick lying in the corner and smashes it over his head as he re-enters the room. But it is not Epihodoff she strikes, it is Lopahin come back from the auction.

As everyone flutters about Lopahin for the news, Gayeff comes in crying and exhausted. Lyuboff begs Lopahin for the news. "Is the cherry orchard sold?" "It's sold." "Who bought it?" "I bought it."

Lopahin tells how the auction went and suddenly cannot resist his gloating triumph. "I bought the estate where grandfather and father were slaves, where you wouldn't even let me in the kitchen. . . .Come on, everybody, and see how Yermolay Lopahin will swing the ax on the cherry orchard, how the trees will fall to the ground!"

Lopahin swaggers a bit and orders the music to "play up." Lyuboff, left alone in the drawing room, cries bitterly. Anya comes in and tries to comfort her: "We will plant a new orchard, finer than this one."

Comment

Directors have frequently interpreted Lopahin's triumphant strutting at the end of the act as an indication that he is a moustache-twirling type of villain. But Chekhov did not envision him that way at all. In a letter to Stanislavsky, he instructed:

"Lopahin is a merchant, of course, but he is a very decent person in every sense. He must behave with perfect decorum, like an educated man, with no petty ways or tricks of any sort."

Lopahin is nearly as startled by the turn of events as is the rest of the household. He has not been secretly planning all along to bid for the estate. His ecstasy at having been the highest bidder for the land on which his father and grandfather were slaves is as moving as the misery which it causes Mme. Ranevskaya. Lopahin's mercantile visions for the orchard: "We are going to build villas and our grandsons and great-grandsons will see a new life here-" are no less laudable than Lyuboff's dreams of selfishly preserving the beauty of her childhood memories.

Chekhov does not take sides here, and to interpret Lopahin as a villain is to mistake the playwright's intention. There are two forces, two visions at work, one must give way to the other. Neither is perfect. Lopahin is incapable of appreciating the peace and natural harmony of the orchard in bloom. For him it represents his family's enslavement. Lopahin has his eyes on the future. People from the city will want summer cottages to enjoy their new leisure, and Lopahin will provide them with their cottages. Many will learn to enjoy the country retreat which once was the privilege of a very few.

Lyuboff cannot care for these many. It is her orchard, her life, which has been sold. Although the estate has gone to waste, and the cherries no longer ripen, the orchard is yet beautiful. Lyuboff cannot part with this beauty or the way of life it represents.

Chekhov presents these two opposing forces with no intended judgment. Each has its merits and faults. Lopahin has no sense of the natural beauty he will destroy, no understanding of the graceful, leisured life it embodies. And yet he is moving with the times. He is a man of the middle-class future, with all its vigor and aesthetic grossness. Lyuboff, emotional, educated, generous, cannot envision this future. She values the beauty and the grace. Here is the predicament. Chekhov offers no easy solution. A lesser dramatist would have made Lopahin an out-and-out villain, thus providing a conventionally maudlin drama of those dispossessed in a period of transition. Chekhov does not allow us such an easy way out. We must face the gigantic dilemma much as it must be faced in real life. Nothing is all good or all bad - all happy or all sad, and whichever side we choose, we will find much that is to our dissatisfaction.

The structure of the act, leading up to Lopahin's entrance is much like a **burlesque** injected with sudden moments of poignancy and truth. The ridiculous "ball" with the postman and railroad clerk as reluctant guests, Charlotta's vaudeville tricks, Trofimoff's slapstick fall down the stairs, Varya's cracking Lopahin accidentally on the head - all these lend an air of chaos and farce. But mixed in with the hubbub are moving confessions: Lyuboff's feeling of doom that today her fate will be decided; Varya's humiliation that for two years people have been waiting for her to marry Lopahin and he has not even proposed; Lyuboff's confrontation with Trofimoff - her misguided heart versus his unfeeling intellectuality.

With Lopahin's announcement the hectic charade finishes. Everyone leaves. The battle has been decided. Lyuboff, left alone in the deserted drawing room, weeps. But Anya's comfort has after all much truth in it: "Mama, you've your life still left you, you've your good, pure heart ahead of you."

Chekhov, then, does not allow Mme. Ranevskaya to be tragic even at her darkest moment. She does still have her life and her health, it is after all only her residence which must change, and she has a pure heart, misguided of course, but yet pure and generous. The loss of her orchard is not, in the end, the loss of her life.

ACT IV

Setting: The same setting as Act I (a room that is still called the nursery). There are neither curtains on the windows nor are there any pictures on the walls. Only a little furniture remains piled up in one corner as if for sale. A sense of emptiness is felt. Near the outer door is a pile of suitcases. The denuded room is busy with activity and the hum of people preparing to leave.

It is October. Two months have passed since Lopahin bought the estate, and everyone is preparing to leave. Lopahin, worn out with "dilly-dallying" around the country, is off to Kharkov on business. Trofimoff is returning to Moscow to take some more courses at the University. Gayeff has accepted a position in a bank (which no one thinks he will keep very long). Anya is going to stay in town and study for the high school examination. She dreams of passing her future evenings reading "lots of books." Varya is going to a town seventy miles away to be a housekeeper. And Lyuboff (with Yasha in tow) is returning to Paris with the money from the Yaroslavl great-aunt. Arrangements have been made to send sick old Fiers to a hospital and Yasha in charge of his departure, announces he has already been sent.

Lopahin has bought a bottle of champagne to celebrate the multiple departures. But no one will have a drink with him. Trofimoff, who anxiously searches for a pair of misplaced rubbers, stops to preach at Lopahin: "Cure yourself of that habit - of arm waving. And also of building summer cottages. . . . Just the same, however, I like you. You have delicate soft fingers like an artist, you have a delicate soft heart."

Lopahin offers Trofimoff some money for his trip. But the student turns pompous again and rejects it: "I am a free man. And everything that you all value so highly and dearly, both rich man and beggars, has not the slightest power over me."

As the two men talk the sound of an ax on a tree is heard in the distance. Anya immediately appears: "Mama begs of you until she's gone, not to cut down the orchard." Lopahin complies, muttering: "What people, really!"

Gayeff and Lyuboff move around the house saying goodbye to their old memories. They are not, after all, so terribly depressed. Gayeff chirps gaily: "Yes, indeed, everything is fine now. Before the sale of the cherry orchard, we all were troubled, distressed, and then when the question was settled definitely, irrevocable, we all calmed down and were even cheerful." Lyuboff agrees: "Yes. My nerves are better . . . I sleep well."

Into the departure preparations bursts Pishtchik, breathless and elated: "Some Englishmen came and found on my land some kind of white clay." Pishtchik has leased them the land for twenty-four years and now has a great deal of money. He is running about the countryside paying off his debts.

As train time grows very near, Lyuboff says she has only two worries. First, that Fiers is sick -but she is reassured that Yasha has sent him to the hospital that morning. And second, that Varya is withering from her lack of activity. Lopahin, with little persuasion, agrees to propose to Varya. But when they are left alone, Lopahin talks of the weather and Varya of a broken thermometer. The moment passes and the proposal never comes.

With a final farewell to the house, the entire entourage leaves. The last one to go is Lopahin, who securely locks every window and door.

Then follows a sad and surprising stage direction: "The stage is empty. You hear the keys locking all the doors, then the carriages drive off. It grows quiet. In the silence you hear the dull thud of an ax on a tree, a lonely, mournful sound. Footsteps are heard. From the door on the right Fiers appears. He is dressed as usual, in a jacket and a white waistcoat, slippers on his feet. He is sick."

Fiers realizes he has been forgotten, and fretting that Gayeff has not put on his heavy coat he lies down on a sofa, muttering to himself: "You haven't got any strength, nothing is left-nothing." He lies very still. The only sound then is the thud of an ax on a tree, far away in the orchard.

Comment

The last moments of *The Cherry Orchard* are startling and extremely moving. Only a brilliant dramatist would have conceived of Fiers' "imprisonment."

For the most part, the last act moves along with an air of bustle and excitement. Everyone has found somewhere to go and appears to be pleased to be going. For Lopahin and Pishtchik the ending is entirely happy. Gayeff looks forward with excitement to his job at the bank. Lyuboff is presumably returning to her lover, that stone around her neck she cannot live without. Anya looks forward dreamily to a life of study and knowledge.

Trofimoff is returning to his perpetual studies. We feel satisfied. The transition has not been so terrible after all. The sense of doom prevailing since the first act is now cleared up and no one has been too badly hurt. Then suddenly Fiers stumbles in - the living embodiment of the superannuated past. And with a great stab of pain we realize it has not been so easy after all.

An entire way of life and the thousands of people who lived it are falling beneath the ax. What will they do with themselves? How will they live? Gayeff will never be able to keep that job; how will he support himself when he loses it? When Lyuboff's lover dies or turns her out again on what will she focus her life? Varya, who dreamed of nunnery, will wither away in another province serving as a housekeeper. Anya, with a full life ahead of her, surely cannot spend all her time reading books. How will she pass her days and nights?

The predicament is not readily soluble, and Chekhov will not give us any easy answers. As the critic John Gassner says: "Checkhov maintained a sensitive equilibrium between regret for the loss of old values and jubilation over the dawn of a new day. And it is the quality of detachment that also enabled him to equalize pathos and humor, and to render a probing account of the contradictions of human character."

As his last play, *The Cherry Orchard* is Chekhov's final statement on a new dramatic method. It is a play of indirect action - nothing happens on the stage. Whatever action there is, is reported. And even the final "shot," which Chekhov could not resist in earlier plays, becomes a faraway sound of axes on trees. The play is devoid of melodrama, external action, and easy answers, and yet it absorbs, excites, provokes a tension common to melodramatic thrillers with contrived twists. All this Chekhov accomplished through absorbing characterization, thick-textured character counterpoint, and a presentation of an insoluble life problem.

ANALYSIS OF SELECTED CHARACTERS

Ranevskaya

Lyuboff is a woman growing old in a world she does not recognize. According to Chekhov she is "an old woman, wholly of the past, with nothing in her of the present." She is utterly foolish in her profligate generosity. No matter how dire her straits, she is ever "the soft touch." As much as Lyuboff cherishes the old house, once it is sold she feels greatly relieved to be freed of the anxiety it causes her.

Life has not treated Lyuboff gently. She has lost husband, son, lover, fortune, and home. But she survives rather well, devoting herself to love and sentiment. Lyuboff is a good and gentle woman, not unintelligent, but somehow out of touch with reality. She is surely more to be pitied than censured as a surrogate of a superannuated society.

Lopahin

In the rich merchant we find the embodiment of the new man, the man of the future. He not only is devoid of sentiment, he is too busy for love. The orchard, with its glorious past, means nothing to him and the sooner he can get the ax to it, the better.

Lopahin is in no sense cruel or heartless. He sympathizes with the family's distress (though he cannot empathize with it), and he wishes he could help them, or that they would not be so foolish. He is a gentleman, educated and decorous. Sensitive about his serf origins, he delights in the pride he brings to his ancestors by the purchase of the estate. He is loved by a religious and honorable woman, and this in itself is a measure of his worth.

Gayeff

Gayeff is sentimental, garrulous, good-natured, and slightly old-maidish. He must constantly be reminded to stop talking so much, and he is still fussed over by Fiers as though he were a young child. Gayeff has never worked and has never been married - he is untouched by responsibility. His great passion is billiards and he plays imaginary games incessantly. Like so many men of his generation, he is educated, genteel, but unable to find anything whatsoever to do with his life.

Trofimoff

Unlike Lopahin, who is building for the future, Trofimoff talks about the future. He has grandiose and visionary views of what the ideal society will be like, but for himself he has yet to take part in its evolution. The perpetual student, taking cover behind his books, Trofimoff has yet to plunge into life. He is "above love," above generosity and sentiment, and he has no patience with human foibles. He is a harsh spokesman at a time when action and gentleness is required.

Varya

The adopted daughter is a strange mixture. She is obsessed and tyrannical about the running of the estate. She bursts into tears or angry tirades with little provocation. She loves Lopahin and is humiliated by his indifference and yet at the same time she cherishes her religious dreams of escape to a nunnery. Varya is not very likeable. She is neither gentle and charming like her sister, not prepared for the future like Lopahin.

ESSAY QUESTIONS AND ANSWERS

Question: How is the cherry orchard used as a symbol?

Answer: When the orchard was in bloom at the height of its productivity, it was a source of great income for its rich owner (and a source of drudgery for the owners' serfs). At one time the orchard represented the possession of human souls for private gain - an ugly emblem of the days of slavery.

After the emancipation, the orchard's productivity waned. The formula for drying the cherries was lost, crops came in only every other year, and when they did ripen they were unsellable. At this point the orchard stood for a foundering society, a society forbidden slavery but unable to function without it. The trees still bore their blossoms, however, and those who could no longer live from their profit could dwell on their beauty. During the days of unproductive blooming, the orchard served as a memory of the old, leisured, well-ordered, moneyed day and provided a source of great visual beauty.

A thing no longer productive cannot survive forever in a progressing world. So as the emancipated generation grows to manhood the relics of their enslavement must be cut down to make room for the new order. The orchard at the end stands for all the things which must fall in the name of progress (and all the values - good and bad - which fall with them). The rising generations, not as refined as the old masters, will be vigorous, hardworking, productive. That the new generation will destroy the natural beauties belonging to one man in order to accommodate not so beautifully many men is unaesthetic but probably necessary. At any rate, as the trees fall someone will suffer: in this case the residents of Gayeff's estate.

Question: How does Chekhov make use of "invisible" characters?

Answer: There are two important members of the cast who are never seen on stage nor mentioned in the program. One is the rich old aunt from Yaroslavl and the other is Mme. Ranevskaya's lover.

Without the aunt, Gayeff and Lyuboff would have had to abandon hope early in Act I. But given a slight possibility of some miracle, they continue to manufacture dreams and avoid action. Had the aunt not sent the 15,000 roubles, they would never even have thought of bidding at the auction and might, with no alternative at all, have listened to Lopahin. As it was, the aunt provided hope and then alternative, the two preventives of action.

Lyuboff's lover is vital as a source of bankruptcy and cause for her absence for so many years. The play is structured around Lyuboff's arrival and departure and the selfish, unhealthy lover provides a motivation for both.

CRITICAL COMMENTARY

There is a surprising dearth of critical material on Chekhov in English. Most of the translations have short introductions, generally biographical, which do little to illuminate Chekhov's craft and philosophy. Since so little is written about Chekhov as playwright, there is practically no critical controversy. The only disagreement among critics concerns Chekhov's final world view: was he a judging moralist, a bright optimist, or a black pessimist? Following is a very brief summary of what four eminent scholars of the drama have said about Chekhov's plays.

ERIC BENTLEY

In his book, *In Search of Theatre*, Eric Bentley uses *Uncle Vanya* as a springboard for a critical chapter on Chekhov. In the commercial theatre Chekhov has a reputation for being "plotless, monotonous, drab and intellectual." Those rebels who produce Chekhov love him, but it "is another question whether they understand him."

In trying to understand Chekhov, Bentley examines the difference between *Uncle Vanya* and the earlier version, *The Wood Demon*. The changes tell a great deal about Chekhov's craft.

First of all, "Chekhov's theatre, like Ibsen's, is psychological," and to keep his characters true he unsettles their previously settled fates.

Chekhov has created his own form of tragic recognition. In his plays "the terrible thing is that the surface of everyday life is itself a kind of tragedy ... the crust [of life's surface] is all too firm; the volcanic energies of men have no chance of emerging."

Chekhov portrayed "the average mediocre men." His characters are, like all men, "very weak" but they have "elements of protest and revolt in them." The sustaining point of his plays is that "these weeping, squirming, suffering creatures might have been men." Chekhov's view is not a misanthropic one because his characters had the potential of fulfillment. The tension in his plays comes from their failure to fulfill this potential.

While the tension comes in nonfulfillment, the motion of the plays comes in the leaking out of narrative and situation - the "progress from ignorance to knowledge." People who label Chekhov's plays as undramatic are only seeing the tininess of the surface movements and "do not notice the enormousness of the forces released."

ROBERT BRUSTEIN

In a forward to an edition of Chekhov's plays (which is adapted from a chapter in his book, *The Theater of Revolt*), the teacher and critic Robert Brustein sees the mature plays as revolts against the "encroaching mediocrity, vulgarity, and illiteracy of Russian life." Chekhov valued above all the gentleness of culture (which is not to be confused with arid intellectuality). "If he is aggrieved by any general fact of Russian life, it is the cancerous growth of slovenliness, filth, stupidity and cruelty among the mass of men; and if he despises the sluggishness and indolence of his upper-class characters, then this is because they, too, are gradually being overwhelmed by the tide, lacking the will to stem it."

The conflict between the forces of light and the forces of darkness provides the "basic substance of most of Chekhov's plays." Brustein describes Chekhov as a moralist and a realist: a realist in the sense that he will not present life as it should be or might be, but in all its tedium as it is; and a moralist in that he criticizes and satirizes on a level beneath the realism.

Although Chekhov eschews melodrama as unnatural, the subsurface of his plays are built around a highly melodramatic pattern - "the conflict between a despoiler and his victims . . . the gradual dispossession of the victims from their rightful inheritance."

JOHN GASSNER

John Gassner, the famous critic and anthologist, sees in Chekhov a great optimist. The playwright never lost his faith in man and "for him there were no failures, even if few of his characters succeed in the world or integrate themselves."

Each of Chekhov's characters has secret longings which reveal "a hidden power to beautify and ennoble life." Although his characters are neither revolutionists nor moralists, they are "always alone."

Chekhov's concept of tragedy departs from the classic and romantic concepts. For him, tragedy is not a clash between individuals but the gradual wearing a way of life. And yet, while the characters are submerged they are not passive. "They dream, they rebel, and they reach out for what they want." Chekhov's characters "attract us by their aliveness, and life is justified and exalted by them."

DAVID MAGARSHACK

In the standard, full-length critical book on Chekhov's plays, David Magarshack asserts that the dramas can be divided into two categories, plays of direct action and plays of indirect action.

The plays of direct action, the early plays up to and through *Ivanov* (1887), follow the conventional pattern of fast-moving, action-filled farces and vaudevilles. But by the time he wrote *The Seagull* (1896) Chekhov had fully developed his "life as it is" theory.

Magarshack describes in great detail the mechanics of Chekhov's indirect-action method. He shows how the active plot is submerged in favor of a total psychological **realism**. He chronicles the uses of chorus, the messenger elements, and the reversals and architecture of each of the plays.

Magarshack's indirect action theory has been accepted and elaborated upon by today's critics. But his insistence that Chekhov's mature plays were dramas of "courage and hope," and that his world view was optimistic, has found few proponents. Magarshack feels that Chekhov's "life as it is" attempts were in fact "life as it should be" lessons, the at Checkhov was pointing an optimistic way to a brighter future.

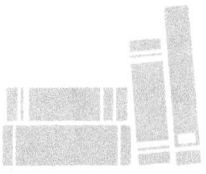

BIBLIOGRAPHY

Translations

Dunnigan, Ann (translator), *Chekhov: the Major Plays* (New York, 1964). This edition of the plays has an insightful and original essay on the plays by the drama critic and scholar Robert Brustein. The translations are not necessarily the best available, but the foreword is of great value.

Yarmolinsky, Avrahm (editor), *The Portable Chekhov* (New York, 1947). A competent selection of short stories and plays with a thorough biographical introduction by Yarmolinsky.

Young, Stark (translator), *Best Plays by Chekhov* (New York, 1956). The best English version of Chekhov's four last plays translated by one of America's greatest critics of the theater.

Letters And Papers

Friedland, Louis (editor), *Chekhov's Letters on the Short Story, the Drama, and Other Literary Topics* (New York, 1964). An excellent collection of letters which reveal the agony and tolerance of a highly serious writer wrestling with his craft.

The Personal Papers of Anton Chekhov (with an introduction by Matthew Josephson, New York, 1948). A limited but highly interesting collection of selections from the notebooks, diary, and letters of Chekhov, filled with essential material on Chekhov's thought on life, literature, and the drama.

Biography

Gorky, Maxim, "Reminiscences of Chekhov," in *1860-1960 A. P. Chekhov* (Moscow, 1960). A perceptive and fascinating memoir of his friend by Chekhov's younger contemporary, Maxim Gorky. Very helpful for its brief but excellent characterization of Chekhov the man and his outlook on life.

Magarshack, David, *Chekhov: A Life* (London, 1952). A scholarly and valuable biography, by an expert in Russian literature and author of a full-length study of Chekhov's plays.

Simmons, Ernest, *Chekhov: A Biography* (Boston, 1962). A massive critical biography, the result of years of research, that is certain to remain the most detailed life of Chekhov.

Criticism

Bentley, Eric, *In Search of Theater* (New York, 1953). Contains an essay called "Craftsmanship in *Uncle Vanya*," a perceptive and suggestive study of Chekhov's stagecraft and vision of life that focuses on *Uncle Vanya* but applies to all the major plays.

Bruford, W. H., *Anton Chekhov* (London, 1957). A brief but balanced and knowledgeable treatment of the plays and stories.

____*Chekhov and His Russia* (London, 1947). A valuable study of the intellectual, social, political, and cultural aspects of Russia that influenced the life and thought of Chekhov.

Gerhardi, W., *Anton Chekhov: A Critical Study* (New York, 1923). One of the earliest studies in English of Chekhov by a sensitive, impressionistic critic. Very interesting for its appreciation of Chekhov, but not very useful for studies of specific works.

Magarshack, David, *Chekhov the Dramatist* (New York, 1960). A full-length critical study of Chekhov's plays. It is the standard critical work on Chekhov, but Magarshack tends to overlook the subtle ironies of Chekhov's vision in favor of fitting all the works into a theory he has formulated.

Stanislavsky, Constantin, *My Life in Art* (New York, 1956). This famous story of the Moscow Art Theater by its celebrated director includes important essays on each of Chekhov's four final plays.